CLINGING
TO
GRANDEUR

Recent Titles in
Contributions to the Study of World History

Disputed Pleasures: Sport and Society in Preindustrial England
Thomas S. Henricks

Origins of Muslim Consciousness in India: A World-System Perspective
Syed Nesar Ahmad

The Persistence of Youth: Oral Testimonies of the Holocaust
Josey G. Fisher, editor

The Silent Holocaust: Romania and Its Jews
I. C. Butnaru

Tea in China: The History of China's National Drink
John C. Evans

The Strange Connection: U.S. Intervention in China, 1944-1972
Bevin Alexander

Medieval Games: Sports and Recreations in Feudal Society
John Marshall Carter

Families in Context: A World History of Population
G. Robina Quale

Waiting for Jerusalem: Surviving the Holocaust in Romania
I. C. Butnaru

Israel's Leadership: From Utopia to Crisis
Jacob Abadi

Christopher Columbus and the Portuguese, 1476-1498
Rebecca Catz

CLINGING
TO
GRANDEUR

British Attitudes and Foreign Policy
in the Aftermath of the Second World War

Michael Blackwell

Contributions to the Study of World History, Number 36

Greenwood Press
Westport, Connecticut • London

Library of Congress Cataloging-in-Publication Data

Blackwell, Michael.
   Clinging to grandeur : British attitudes and foreign policy in the
aftermath of the Second World War / Michael Blackwell.
     p.   cm.—(Contributions to the study of world history, ISSN
0885-9159 ; no. 36)
   Includes bibliographical references and index.
   ISBN 0-313-28616-7 (alk. paper)
   1. Great Britain—Foreign relations—1945- 2. Statesmen—Great
Britain—Attitudes. 3. National characteristics, British. 4. World
War, 1939-1945—Influence.   I. Title. II. Series.
DA589.8.B57 1993
327.41—dc20 92-30012

British Library Cataloguing in Publication Data is available.

Library of Congress Catalog Card Number: 92-30012
ISBN: 0-313-28616-7
ISSN: 0885-9159

First published in 1993

Greenwood Press, 88 Post Road West, Westport, CT 06881
An imprint of Greenwood Publishing Group, Inc.

Printed in the United States of America

The paper used in this book complies with the
Permanent Paper Standard issued by the National
Information Standards Organization (Z39.48-1984).

10 9 8 7 6 5 4 3 2 1

Copyright Acknowledgments

The author and publisher gratefully acknowledge permission to quote from the
Alexander and Attlee letters and papers, and speeches.

Extracts from the Alexander papers are published by kind permission of the
Master and Fellows of Churchill College, Cambridge. Excerpts from the
Alexander letters and speeches are published by kind permission of Lady
Beatrix Evison.

Extracts from the Attlee papers are published by kind permission of the Master
and Fellows of University College, Oxford and the Bodleian Library,
University of Oxford. Excerpts from the Attlee letters are published by kind
permission of Lady Attlee.

How often do miscalculations in the statesman,
like narrowness and blunder in the historian,
spring from neglect of the pregnant and
illuminating truth that deeper than men's opinions
are the sentiment and circumstances by which
opinion is predetermined.
(John Morley, *Politics and History*)

Contents

Acknowledgments   ix

Part 1   Elements of the Context   1

  1. Introduction   3
  2. Attitudes and Foreign Policy   9
  3. The Foreign Policy Decision-Making Process   17
  4. Bevin's Relations With His Officials   31

Part 2   The Attitudes of the Policymakers   43

  5. Attitude Formation in Childhood Years   45
  6. Attitude Formation in Later Years   61
  7. Public Opinion   81

Part 3   The Economic Setting   87

  8. Attitudes and the Perception of Britain's Economic Situation   89

**Part 4   The Evolution of Attitudes and Their Significance in
Specific Areas of Foreign Policy**   105

  9. The Evolution of Attitudes and the Search For Prestige   107
10. Attitudes and Specific Policy Issues   115

Part 5   Conclusion   159

11. Clinging to Grandeur   161

Part 6   Select Bibliography   165

Index   193

Acknowledgments

I thank Lord Gladwyn, Lord Shinwell, Sir Nicholas Henderson and Sir Frank Roberts for talking to me about their memories of Ernest Bevin, the Cabinet, and the Foreign Office; and Piers Dixon for making available to me the papers of his father, Sir Pierson Dixon. I am grateful for help received from staff in the following libraries and archives: the University of East Anglia; the Public Records Office, London; University College, Nuffield College, and the Bodleian Library, Oxford; Churchill College, Cambridge; the Imperial War Museum, London; the British Library; *The Times* Archives; and the London School of Economics.

Of the many people who gave me advice and encouragement, I thank particularly Professors Michael Balfour and Paul Kennedy and Dr. Robert Short. I also thank Jay Williams, Jennie Tobler and my son Adam for preparing the manuscript for publication. Finally, I thank my other children, Richard, John, and Tom, and my wife Carole, who all in their own ways helped to make this book possible.

Part 1

Elements of the Context

1

Introduction

The foreign policy decisions taken in Britain in the few years immediately following the Second World War were to have a major impact on the course of the country's history in the remainder of the century. The vigorous pursuit of a major world power role that the country could no longer afford reduced the resources available for reconstruction and development at home and contributed significantly to the country's relative economic decline in the 1950s and to a consequential weakening of its position in the world economy in the decades that were to follow.[1] In studying the foreign and economic policy of the period, there are two basic questions that arise, the answers to which require recourse to psychological as well as to the more general social, political, and economic analyses. First, when the country's economic situation was so much worse than it had been before the war, why did the policymakers adopt foreign policy decisions that were so costly and ambitious?[2] And second, why were these decisions taken by Britain's first majority socialist government? Why, against expectations, did the Labour Party leaders choose to pursue the maintenance and strengthening of the British Empire, to cling on to other costly overseas commitments, and to accept, as a consequence, slower economic development at home?

THE ECONOMY

With regard to the economy, the elation felt by British policymakers at the victorious conclusion of the Second World War was quickly tempered by the realization of the severity of British financial losses during the war and by the acknowledgement that the country's economic performance in the future would have to be much improved over the prewar period merely to restore prewar living standards. Several government papers made clear that Britain was running a large deficit on the current account of its balance of payments, a deficit that was bound to continue for several years into the peace.[3] Compared with a sum of £70 million in 1938, the deficit was expected to rise as high as £750 million in 1946.[4] Prospects for eliminating the current account deficit were worsened by the loss of over 50 percent of the country's prewar shipping tonnage, the loss of export markets, and the damage done to the export industries not only by bombing but also by the reorganization of industry to meet specific wartime needs. To make matters worse, many of the country's overseas investments had been liquidated during the war, and income from that source in 1945 was less than half that received in 1938.

The chance of boosting exports was also undermined by the need to use resources for making good the considerable war damage suffered throughout Britain. Some four million homes had been damaged by enemy action, of which 210 thousand had been totally destroyed and 250 thousand rendered uninhabitable. The total damage to property was estimated at £1,450 million at the prevailing replacement costs. Over and above such losses, industrial capacity had been run down by the deliberate policy of deferring all but the most vital repair and maintenance. During the war the country had not merely lived on its external capital but had also suffered a considerable measure of domestic disinvestment as industrial and other enterprises had been compelled by shortage of materials and labour to allow arrears of normal depreciation and obsolescence to accumulate. Also of significance was the lack of normal maintenance of private residential property and the running down of stocks of clothing and household goods. In 1945 exports had sunk to one third of their prewar level, and the prospects for boosting them to a level 75 percent in excess of the prewar level, which was seen as necessary for the "full restoration of a reliable equilibrium," did not appear hopeful.[5]

The papers made clear that radical measures would be needed to finance the large ongoing current account deficit. It was obvious that the country's reserves could not be used for that purpose. The reserves had sunk below £100 million in 1940 and 1941, and although they had risen after that, largely as a result of the presence of U.S. forces in the country, they stood at only £450 million at the end of the war, a sum less than the estimated level of £864 million in 1938 and considerably less than the projected account deficit for 1946. Moreover, Britain finished the war with greatly increased external liabilities. To prosecute the war not only were overseas capital assets sold or repatriated but massive debts were also incurred. As a result total external debt rose from around £476 million in 1939 to an unprecedented £3,355 million at the close of hostilities.

It was clear that until exports could be boosted sufficiently, and without foreign borrowing, Britain's current account could only be balanced by cutting back on imports or by reducing overseas expenditure. Equally clear was that any failure to restore balance would necessitate further resort to foreign borrowing. Restrictions on imports remained in place for several years after the war, but there was little hope of reducing their absolute level since so much had to be bought from abroad to make possible the industrial regeneration essential for the country's long-term economic health. At 1947 prices, imports in fact rose from £835 million in 1938 to £1,092 million in 1946 and to £1,541 million in 1947.

The authorities were able to borrow from abroad, particularly from the United States and Canada. The supply of money available, however, was not limitless. It was offered with irksome conditions attached, and, of course, the more that Britain accepted, the greater her already alarming level of external debt became. For these reasons, officials at the Treasury stated the need for Britain not only to limit the growth of its overseas expenditure but also to cut it back. Any savings on the more than £500 million[6] spent in maintaining British commitments overseas (compared with £16 million in 1938), they argued, could be used to strengthen the home economy, at the very least by reducing the need for foreign borrowing.[7]

These arguments could have been expected to appeal to the new Labour government whose socialist philosophy could have been expected to favour massive increases in planned government investment at home over the pursuit of great power politics abroad. In fact, the Labour leaders sought energetically to maintain and in some cases to expand Britain's imperial role, and in so doing they used up resources that might otherwise have been allocated to domestic expenditures, notably, the rebuilding of infrastructure and new investment in industry that could have increased the standard of living of working people and built a more solid foundation for future economic growth. Why were the Labour leaders as reluctant to recognize the nation's economic limitations? Why did they continue to pursue an essentially Churchillian Tory foreign policy based on the need to assert world power status through the maintenance of expensive commitments throughout the world?

THE NEW LABOUR GOVERNMENT

A general election was called in 1945, and during the campaign the Conservative leaders tried to remind the electorate of the slogans of socialist internationalism, anti-imperialism, disarmament, and abandonment of balance of power politics, which were portrayed as fundamental socialist beliefs and which had been mouthed by Labour politicians in the years before the war.[8] In a leaflet, "Guilty Men," they pointed to Labour opposition to conscription in the run-up to the war, noting in particular the opposition of the Labour Party leader Clement Attlee in the debate on the Conscription Bill in April 1939. Other pamphlets and leaflets included "Contrast in Records," which contrasted Conservative defence measures and Labour pacifism, and "Your M.P.," a list of Labour Members of Parliament (MPs) who voted against conscription in 1939. It was recalled that in setting out his political philosophy before the war, Attlee had stated clearly that there could be "no agreement on foreign policy between a Labour opposition and a capitalist government."[9]

And yet, when the Labour Party won a convincing victory, and when Attlee, the middle-class academic, and Ernest Bevin, the working-class former trade union leader, came to power as Prime Minister and Foreign Secretary they, together with other party leaders, conducted a foreign policy marked most of all by its continuity with the policy pursued by their Tory predecessors Winston Churchill and Anthony Eden. Far from being anti-imperialist, the Labour Government sought to maintain control over the countries of the British Empire--Indian independence in 1947 was conceded only reluctantly--and even took steps to expand the empire by adding Sarawak to the fold in 1946 against the opposition of the native representatives of the Sarawak Legislative Council. Disarmament was obviously not a high government priority as the Labour leadership sanctioned the development of an independent atomic bomb program for Britain, which was enormously expensive not only in terms of cash but also in terms of opportunity costs in the diversion of scarce materials and energy away from other infrastructural and industrial development. Instead of socialist internationalism and the rejection of balance of power politics, Attlee and, in particular, Bevin continued Churchill's suspiciousness and hostility toward the Soviet Union and sought to maintain a British presence in Greece, throughout the Middle East, and elsewhere east of Suez in order to push the course of events toward the outcome favoured by British interests. These policies and the efforts made to fall in with the policies of the United States triggered revolts among many of the party's backbenchers.[10] In November 1946, 58 Labour Members of Parliament, angered by the drift away from socialist principles in the government's foreign policy, took the unusual move of proposing to Parliament an amendment to their own government's program for the coming year as presented in the king's speech.[11] With what Bevin saw as an element of treachery, the amendment called for a change of direction in foreign policy so as

> to afford the utmost encouragement to and collaboration with all nations and groups striving to secure full socialist planning and control of the world's resources and thus provide a democratic and constructive socialist alternative to an otherwise inevitable conflict between American capitalism and Soviet communism in which all hope of World Government would be destroyed.[12]

While in the vote at the end of the debate, none of those favoring the amendment went so far as to vote against the government, 130 Labour MPs were either absent or abstained from voting. However, neither this revolt from the rank and file nor the growing evidence of the parlous state of the British economy could divert the Labour Government from its chosen course.

To understand how the policymakers--both civil service and political leaders--continued to pursue their vision of British world preeminence amid mounting evidence of the adverse consequences for the home economy, and to understand how socialist politicians could pursue the type of foreign policy they had earlier criticized when practiced by their Conservative predecessors, it is essential to understand the psychological elements of the decision-making process. More specifically, it is necessary to understand the attitudes of these policymakers and the significant role these attitudes played in the formulation and execution of foreign policy decisions.

NOTES

1. For the development of this point see, for example, Balogh (1952) pp. 479-480; Barber (1975) pp. 272-282; Calvacoressi (1978) pp. 199, 202; Darby (1973) p. 55; Dow (1964) p. 25; Frankel (1975) pp. 91-92, and 1971 p. 91; Goldstein (1966) p. 13; Greenwood (1976) pp. 5-26; Kennedy (1976) p. 325; Shonfield (1957) p. 38; Sprout (1963) pp. 655-658; Waltz (1968) p. 178; and Youngson (1967) p. 256.

2. The word *policymakers* is used to designate the political leaders holding office in the Labour government and the senior career officials in the Foreign Office. These individuals are identified later.

3. The statistics in this chapter are taken from two of the most important contemporary government analyses of the economy: *Statistical Material Presented During the Washington Negotiations*, CMD 6707 (December 1945) and the *Economic Survey for 1947* CMD 7046 (February 1947).

4. In fact, due to a better than expected export performance and to difficulties in obtaining imports, the deficit amounted to only £380 million. This, of course, was still a very large sum that required loans from Canada and the United States for its financing.

5. CMD 6707, p. 5.

6. This figure does not include the salaries of the armed forces nor a number of domestic expenditures relating to overseas commitments. Critics of government policy calculated that the total cost of maintaining

overseas commitments was around £2,000 million per annum (see Attlee Papers, Letter from K. Zilliacus to C. R. Attlee, 11 February 1946).

7. See, for example, PRO, CP 45: 112.

8. Fitzsimmons (1950) p. 198.

9. Attlee (1937) pp. 226-227.

10. In the British House of Commons, members with government offices or in the case of the opposition party shadow government offices sit on the front benches of the chamber. Backbenchers are therefore rank-and-file members of each party who have not been named to office.

11. At the beginning of each parliamentary year in the United Kingdom, the monarch officially opens Parliament with a speech that sets out the government's legislative program and objectives.

12. For this text and a discussion of the revolt see Bullock (1983) pp. 327-329.

2

Attitudes and Foreign Policy

Before assessing to what degree policymakers' attitudes might have affected foreign policy decisions taken in the aftermath of the Second World War, it is necessary to define what is meant by attitudes; how they are formed, how they are changed, how they affect behaviour, how they can be identified, and how they should be approached as a tool of historical analysis.

DEFINITION

Defining attitudes is not in fact an easy task. In the field of social psychology there are yet many unresolved battles, and the analysis of attitudes is still one of the most fought-over terrains. An attempt has been made in this chapter to remain within the areas of consensus and to elaborate a basic approach to the concept that both Freudians and behaviourists alike would find unobjectionable. A definition of attitudes that would still win wide acceptance is that of Allport, who defined an attitude as "a mental and neural state of readiness, organized through experience, exerting a directive or dynamic influence upon the individual's response to all objects and situations with which it is related."[1] In other words, attitudes not only represent latent states of preparedness, but are also endowed with motivational qualities and are established through learning and experience.

It would also be widely accepted that attitudes have three basic components, which can be distinguished from each other but are to some degree interdependent.

1. a cognitive component--the way a person *thinks* with regard to an object. Is it good or bad? Appropriate or inappropriate?
2. an affective component--the way a person *feels* with regard to an object. Does he like it or dislike it? Does it make him happy or unhappy?

3.   an action tendency component--the way a person *behaves* with regard
      to an object. Does he make contact or avoid it? Study or ignore it?

Although individuals can live with varying degrees of incongruity between
components of their attitudes towards various objects, it is generally true that any
conflict between attitudinal components has a destabilizing effect on the
personality, and congruity is sought either through direct overt activity or by
symbolic activity.

A person will tend to hold a "constellation" of attitudes; that is, given
his attitude to one object, his attitude to another can often be deduced with
reasonable accuracy. Similar attitude constellations will be held by people with
shared group affiliations; thus, for example, the attitudes of members of a
conservative political party are likely to be different from those of Communist
Party members. The officials of the Foreign Office of the 1940s shared very
similar social and educational backgrounds, and it would not be unreasonable to
expect that they would also share similar attitude constellations.[2]

FORMATION

Attitudes, as Allport's definition clearly stated, are learned. They are
learned in a formal way at schools, colleges, churches, trade union meetings, and
at other institutions, and, in a less formal way, through the press, the cinema,
literature, and other cultural forms. Perhaps most important of all, however,
attitudes are learned as a result of social interaction. A person's attitudes and
behaviour tend to be established in a way that will conform to the expectations
held by members of the groups to which he belongs (peer groups), and perhaps
of even greater importance to those held by members of groups to which he
aspires to belong (reference groups).

These groups, however, are not always well defined. People can, for
instance, feel an identity with a generalized age group. Lord Gladwyn, who
worked in the Foreign Office in the early postwar period, described in his
memoirs how the tendency of the older Foreign Office officials to favour Britain
playing her full part as a great power contrasted with the more modest views of
the younger officials.[3] At an even more diffuse level, people can have a sense
of identity with a national group and will tend to agree with the most commonly
held concepts about their country's role and about international affairs in general.
Evidence of this can be found, for example, in the results of Gallup polls held
simultaneously in different countries.[4]

In the formation of attitudes, it is the years of maturation that are of the
most significance. At one level, a "personality" is the name given to a particular
constellation of attitudes, and once a basic personality is formed, it can be

changed only with difficulty.   Halloran goes so far as to say that "in all probability, once we have thought about ourselves in a certain way, the influence of that particular self conception can never be completely eradicated."[5]

The power of attitudes formed in childhood was commented on by Lord (then Sir Oliver) Franks in his Reith lectures. Franks is perhaps rather more an academic philosopher than a civil servant or diplomat, but after a distinguished wartime record in Whitehall, he was named in 1948 as British Ambassador to the United States and was certainly among those involved in the foreign policy decision-making process.[6] Addressing his radio audience, he remarked:

> The psychologists have told us that sensations and impressions received in very early childhood exercise a determining role in the broad attitudes we have to life in later years. I think in some ways they exaggerate; but not in all. If anyone suddenly says to me "The Map of the World," the picture which instantly rises in my mind is Mercator's projection from my 1912 atlas, with so much of the world coloured in one flat wash red, the many overseas dependencies of Britain, the British Empire. Such vivid associations almost unconsciously colour one's approach to world affairs and the place of Britain.[7]

Lord (then Mr. A. V.) Alexander, a Minister of Defence in Attlee's Cabinet, recalled in a 1946 speech the deep effect of his childhood reading of books by such consciously patriotic writers as Rudyard Kipling and G. A. Henty, and then observed, "I am glad that when the testing time came in May 1940 that I had not rejected what men call platitudes, for in such times the so-called platitudes became a verity of life."[8]

It seems clear from the context of this passage that Alexander is saying that his childhood attitudes towards Britain and her world role found a new resurgence in the test of war. Implicit in his remarks is the suggestion that during the intervening period he may have been tempted to adopt new attitudes in order to conform with postchildhood group affiliations (such as the Labour Party), but that the attitudes established in his youth were never fully replaced.

This point is made more explicitly by Lord Longford, (then Frank Pakenham), a Junior Minister, who worked with Foreign Secretary Ernest Bevin on German affairs. In his memoirs he admitted that in joining the Labour Party he "stoked up a little artificial enthusiasm" for Soviet Russia, but he later makes clear that his transitory excitement did not in any way lead him to suppress his earlier anti-Russian attitudes.[9]

FUNCTIONS

Views on the functions of attitudes vary widely according to the different schools of thought in psychology. However, it is generally accepted that attitudes help to fill the human need for consistency. A person prefers certainty, stability, and consistency rather than uncertainty, instability, and ambiguity. He needs standards or frames of reference for understanding the world, and attitudes help to provide these. This point is well illustrated by Lord Franks, who proposed that the attitude that

> Britain is going to continue to be what she has been, a Great Power. . . is part of the habit and furniture of our minds; a principle so much one with our outlook and character that it determines the way we act without emerging itself into clear consciousness.[10]

The rest of his lecture makes clear that this attitude, which he saw as "part of the habit and furniture" of his own mind, provided a frame of reference in which he made sense of postwar history. If other policymakers shared this same frame of reference, then it follows that in the decision-making process they would have been predisposed to follow those courses of action most likely to maintain Britain's status as a "great power." During Alexander's mission to India in 1946, he found himself at a dinner party in New Delhi, where, as he recalls,

> a good part of the evening resolved itself into an argument about the responsibility for all the things that have happened or are happening in India, which I am afraid rather excited a desire to defend my country. . . I am afraid that I expressed my view on this aspect pretty forcibly. . . even suggesting that it was not a good time, when we were looking for the utmost cooperation and goodwill, for anyone to start crying "stinking fish."[11]

In this incident it is clear that Alexander's reaction to others' questioning of his basic attitudes concerning his country is not to evaluate the criticisms but to reestablish congruity as soon as possible by forcibly denying them. Could this approach, which displays a lack of balanced judgment, have been repeated in the decisions that Alexander took as first Lord of the Admiralty or as Minister of Defence? Sir David Kelly, a Foreign Office official, looking back at foreign policy decisionmakers during this period, said that he had seen many important issues decided by personal likes or dislikes or by mere prejudice--"the men who take the decisions usually rationalize them later."[12]

Ernest Bevin often implied that, when taking decisions, he relied on intuitive feelings (in other words, his attitudes) rather than on weighty expert evaluations. In 1948, for example, he told the miners that

> foreign affairs in the past has [sic] been treated as if they were something over the heads of everybody; they were supposed to be matters for very clever diplomats. Believe me, that is all moonshine. Foreign affairs is commonsense people talking to commonsense people. That is all it amounts to.[13]

CHANGE

Attitudes can be changed. Either the change can be total and immediate or it can affect the different attitudinal components in differing degrees over a long period of time. Attitude change usually takes place, at least at a cognitive level, when there is an irreconcilable conflict, cognitive dissonance, between two cognitions. For example, a person could disbelieve seriously regarded reports of German concentration camps that emerged during the war but would find it impossible to do so when film and other incontrovertible evidence became available toward the end of the hostilities. In other words, there comes a point when a previously held cognition must give way. It should not be forgotten, however, as Halloran has pointed out, that dissonance situations do not always produce dissonance-reducing behaviour. As will be discussed later, individuals often have a surprising capacity to live with dissonance.

The major explanation of attitude stability lies in a person's group affiliations:

> Research shows quite clearly that attitudes which have strong social support through group affiliations are difficult to change. If a person values his membership in a group he will tend to cling to the attitudes endorsed by that group in order to maintain his status and position.[14]

As the next chapter will explain, the Foreign Office officials of the late 1940s formed a distinct elite group sharing common backgrounds and a clear sense of group identity. It would follow from Halloran's proposition that the members of this elite would tend to share similar attitudes, particularly with regard to Britain and her world role, since they worked together in that field. The pressures to maintain certain attitudes would have been felt by all members of the group and also by any individuals who made of the Foreign Office officials a reference group. It will be shown later that Ernest Bevin, in spite of his different social background, did just this.

CONCLUSIONS AND METHODOLOGICAL CONSIDERATIONS

An attitude can be understood as the way in which one views an object or a concept. Attitudes are learned throughout life, but those learned during maturation tend to be enduring and resistant to change. Attitudes act as a frame of reference that can be used to give order and logic to the whole array of facts and other stimuli that impinge upon the individual. Attitudes play an important part in the determination of behavioural responses to these facts and stimuli. Individuals tend to make efforts to ensure that their attitudes conform to the attitudes generally held by other individuals in peer and reference groups. No decision-making process can be adequately comprehended, therefore, without an understanding of the attitudes of the individuals participating in the process.

Using attitudes as the central theme of a piece of historical research creates certain problems. Firstly, attitudes, being mental and neural states, are not available for direct study as are, for example, international treaties or balance-of-payments statistics. As Kierkegaard remarked, "The results, the consequences of actions are there to be seen; the causes, the motives are hidden in men's minds, and only God can disentangle them."[15] Without divine omniscience, the historian can only hope to deduce attitudes from the writings, sayings, and actions of those he is studying. The obvious danger here is that the researcher's own attitudes will influence his perception and analysis of this evidence. This danger is unavoidable, and constant efforts have to be made to minimize it by being aware of its existence and by maintaining a determination to record views that do not accord with an original hypothesis.

A second problem is that decisionmakers might have taken conscious steps to conceal or disguise their real attitudes. It is rather troubling, for example, to note that at a Cabinet meeting in December 1945, Attlee, suggested that ministers should, as far as was possible, avoid asking that dissenting views that they had expressed in Cabinet be specially recorded in the minutes of the Cabinet's proceedings.[16] This injunction was obviously intended to reduce the damage caused by leaks. It meant for the future historian, however, that much evidence of differing attitudes and opinions would be hidden under such bland phrases as "a discussion ensued." The problem of an incomplete record applies not only to the politicians but also to the Foreign Office officials. In diplomacy, it has always been believed advisable to keep some assumptions resolutely unspoken. Thus, during an exchange of ideas in 1946, in which it becomes apparent that the Foreign Office was in favour of the creation of a Western bloc in Europe, Sir Nigel Ronald, an Assistant Under-Secretary of State, wrote:

We should, however, refrain for the present from any public statement that this is our intention. Rather we should for the present keep the idea to ourselves and allow it to impose itself by force of circumstance on the minds of others.[17]

Not only are attitudes hidden, but there are occasions when alien attitudes are expressed for a particular reason; for example, to boost morale at home or to improve the country's image abroad. Grant McKenzie, an information officer in the British Embassy at Washington in 1946, advised all British officials abroad to talk only of the successes of the Labour government, to "use the language of idealism whenever possible to whip up interest and enthusiasm on the lines of war-time practice."[18]

Great care has to be taken not to be swayed by this type of artificial optimism that was resorted to even by distinguished thinkers such as Lord Keynes. In 1938, a month before the Munich Conference, he wrote to a friend, Kingsley Martin, concerning Anglo-German relations: "I agree with you that we should bluff to the hilt, and if the bluff is called, back out. I prefer meanwhile meiosis and bogus optimism in public."[19] Should this admission affect the researcher's interpretation of Keynes's important speeches in 1945 and 1946?

In an attempt to overcome problems of this nature, efforts have been made in this study to balance any publicly made speeches or statements with those made in personal letters and other private papers. The contrast between private and public views is evident in the writings of Hugh Dalton, the Chancellor of the Exchequer from 1945 to 1947, whose speeches display much greater patriotism and optimism than do the entries in his diary. (Here yet one more caveat is in order: many diaries were written with a future public audience in mind.) Efforts have also been made to cross reference wherever possible; for example, with regard to Cabinet meetings, it has been instructive to compare accounts that were written up in various diaries with the official account recorded by the Cabinet Secretariat.

Finally, this study focuses on the attitudes of the policymakers as they were expressed in the years immediately following the Second World War. It is probable that these attitudes might have been somewhat different at other stages of the policymakers' lives; particularly, for example, during the depths of the depression in the 1930s. While a chronological study of the evolution of attitudes over time would be fascinating, what is of importance for this study is not so much how the political and economic events of earlier periods were perceived at the time they were taking place as how these events were perceived and how these perceptions were embodied in attitudes during the specific period under review, i.e., during the early years of the first Attlee government.

NOTES

1. Quoted in Halloran (1967) p. 14.

2. The attitude constellations concerning the world role of one's country have been classified by some international relations theorists as "strategic images". See Frankel (1973) pp. 71-74.

3. Gladwyn (1972) pp. 111-117.

4. See several examples in Gallup (1972).

5. Halloran (1967) p. 37.

6. Many British Government ministries are located in Whitehall, London; *Whitehall* is commonly used as a synonym for government services.

7. Franks (1954) p. 807.

8. Alexander Papers, Speech at dinner of the Printers' Pension Almshouse and Orphan Asylum Corporation, 12 November 1946.

9. Pakenham (1953) p. 80.

10. Franks (1954) p. 788; see also Frankel (1973) p. 72. There is much experimental evidence to show the existence of a general human tendency to fit incoming stimuli into a desired pattern or *Gestalt*; see for example Gregory (1966).

11. Alexander papers, File AVAR 28/3.

12. Kelly (1953) pp. 1-2.

13. National Union of Miners Conference Report, (1948) p. 117.

14. Halloran (1967) p. 60.

15. Quoted in Beloff (1970) p. 7.

16. Public Records Office (hereafter PRO) CM (45) 58, (3 December 1945).

17. PRO, FO/371/59911, Z2410/120/72 (13 March 1946).

18. Attlee Papers, Letter to Attlee, 30 January 1946.

19. Letter to Kingsley Martin, 1938, quoted in McLachlan (1971) p. 151.

3

The Foreign Policy
Decision-Making Process

Britain's foreign policy decision-making process is easier to describe for the immediate post-Second World War years than it is for the 1990s. Understanding foreign policy decision making in contemporary Britain involves examination of the interrelationship of the Foreign Office with numerous other entities such as other departments of state, international organizations, and economic pressure groups. The complexity of the decision-making process reflects the increasingly complicated nature of the world environment where international, intergovernmental organizations continue to proliferate and technological change continues apace. Some of this complexity can, however, be attributed to the decline in Britain's world power, which has meant that economic and commercial objectives have become major foreign policy preoccupations. In this setting, the practice of a relatively pure foreign policy in the Palmerstonian manner is no longer possible.[1]

In the years immediately following the Second World War, however, the situation was somewhat different. Obviously, groups such as the military Chiefs of Staff or officials at the Treasury had definite views on world affairs that were not without influence, but the greatest weight in foreign policy making still lay with the Foreign Secretary and his Foreign Office officials. Indeed, this period is one of the last in which the Cabinet and the Foreign Office had such preponderant voices in making foreign policy decisions.[2] This chapter looks at the leading members of these two institutions and describes their relationship in the decision-making process.

THE FOREIGN OFFICE

In the mid-1940s, Foreign Office officials could generally be characterized by the similarity of their social backgrounds, by their public school/Oxbridge education, by the club atmosphere in which they worked, and by their conservative view of working methods and indeed of foreign relations in general.[3] The following list of nineteen officials includes the most senior Foreign Office positions, the Ambassadors to the United States and the Soviet Union, and those working directly for Ernest Bevin immediately after the war:

F.T.A. Ashton-Gwatkin
N. M. Butler
Sir Alexander Cadogan
J.I.C. Crombie
P. Dixon
H. M. Gladwyn Jebb
E. L. Hall Patch
O. C. Harvey
R. G. Howe
Sir A. K. Clark Kerr
I. A. Kirkpatrick
M. D. Peterson
N. B. Ronald
Sir Orme Sargent
D.J.M.D. Scott
Sir William Strang
A. J. Toynbee
C.F.A. Warner
C. K. Webster

No fewer than fifteen of these had been to Oxford or Cambridge; the same number had received early education at a public school of the Headmasters' Conference. Of those remaining, not one had been educated at a regular state school. The social homogeneity of this group was maintained by the recruitment procedures in force during the first two decades of this century when these men had joined the Foreign Office. For example, at that time, no applicant could have been considered for the Diplomatic Service unless he had an assured income of £400 per annum,[4] and the entrance examinations themselves were set in a way that favoured Oxbridge candidates.[5] The result was that the Foreign Office remained, in the words of one senior member, "a closely knit body of officials who knew each other very well both in the office and in their social relations outside."[6]

The Second World War and the attempts to widen access to employment in the Foreign Office implemented by Anthony Eden during the course of the war did, it is true, bring some changes to the recruitment procedure, but it was a long time before they brought about any noticeable change in the social composition and unity of the staff; for example, of the 250 candidates accepted between 1945 and 1950, as many as 180 had been educated at a public school of the Headmasters' Conference.[7] One contemporary official, John Connell, observed that in spite of everything, after the Second World War, "the essential qualities of the office survived. . . so did the spirit in which it conducted its affairs."[8]

This spirit was made manifest in the officials' evident desire to uphold the traditional form of diplomacy based on the gentlemanly virtues taught by the Edwardian public schools. Economics and public relations were often seen as vulgar modernisms, and there was a general repugnance for what was seen as the unsophisticated diplomacy of the Americans. F.T.A. Ashton-Gwatkin, a senior official, gave expression to these feelings to an American university audience in 1949. Explaining how economic power had become of increasing importance in international relations, he declared that the British Foreign Office had "*perforce* and *reluctantly* developed its organs for dealing with economic intelligence." He then went on to speak about public relations:

> In addition, the Foreign Service has reluctantly recognized the importance of the new strategic technique of publicity and ideology. The work of the information services and of the British Council is evidence of this. But we are not very good publicists, and I would expect that much of this new annex to the Foreign Service would be sacrificed to the first big demand for economy.[9]

Changes of this nature meant that the British style of diplomacy drew closer to that of the Americans, and this was difficult to accept. One official commenting on this change in mid-1945 must have spoken for many colleagues: "It is hard for us to adjust ourselves to this change. It means for us the abandonment or at least the modification of gentlemanly reticence to which we have clung so far."[10] The distrust of economics and the need to conform to a certain gentlemanly ethic are a reflection of the social and educational background that the Foreign Office staff shared.

The working methods of the Foreign Office at this time have been described by a former Permanent Secretary, Lord Strang.[11] He explained how incoming information was received by one of the numerous individuals at the base of the pyramid-like structure and was then transmitted up the pyramid with minutes and tentative proposals for action given at each stage by the appropriate official. Ultimately, it reached the Permanent Under-Secretary, who confirmed or, in some cases suggested, the course of action to be taken. Final approval would be given by the Secretary of State. The great bulk of Foreign Office business was taken up with considered responses to *faits accomplis*. Nevertheless, there were occasions in which British policymakers tried to take the initiative in world affairs, particularly during Bevin's early days at the office. One of his first actions was, for example, to gather the leading officials together and request that they elaborate and execute a policy that would improve the lot of the poor masses of the Middle East. However, officials spent so much time assimilating and reacting to events arising in the external environment that they had little left to give to such questions of principle. In any case, Foreign Office officials, grounded as they were in the British empirical tradition, felt much easier working with the *fait accompli*. George Young recalled the sighs of relief in Whitehall when another party took the initiative, even if it was to Britain's disadvantage. The relief was occasioned by the officials' knowledge that there were, at last, solid facts to work on.[12]

Duff Cooper, Ambassador to France at the time but not a career Foreign Office man, got on well with the French bureaucracy because he was willing to consider questions theoretically and not solely on an *a posteriori* empirical basis. "Il parle de principes, ce qui est rare chez un anglais," one French civil servant wrote.[13] The Foreign Office in London was, however, often uneasy about Cooper's work, and some of his more radical recommendations for an innovative British foreign policy were politely noted for the record and left pending *sine die*. Meanwhile, the Foreign Office continued working on what Lord Strang was to term the compelling nature of events in international life.[14]

Another way of illustrating the official preference for facts over principles would be to compare the relative success of various interdepartmental committees set up after the war. Those that dealt with specific questions, such as the steering committee on international organizations, set up in 1946, met frequently and seemed to achieve their objectives efficiently. Those such as the committee set up by Bevin to consider long-term aspects of foreign policy met infrequently and made no contributions of value to the policy-making process.[15]

THE CABINET

In considering the role of the Cabinet, it should first be noted that its foreign policy decisions become acts of State, and unless substantial sums of money are involved, no parliamentary approval for them is required. One practical consequence of this fact is that in Cabinet meetings the decisions of the Foreign Secretary tend to be less extensively scrutinised than those of his colleagues with domestic responsibilities. This was particularly true during the first few years of the Attlee Cabinet, when the foreign policy decisions were left almost exclusively in the hands of the Prime Minister and Foreign Secretary. This can largely be explained by two facts: firstly, on the home front the tremendous work-load carried by the government ministers in the aftermath of war meant that they had insufficient time to brief themselves adequately on external affairs; and secondly, even if they had had the time, they would have had little inclination because of Bevin's dominant status in the group. In many respects his power was even greater than that of the Prime Minister. As Emmanuel (later Lord) Shinwell, a member of the Attlee cabinet, recalled, "during that period we left foreign affairs to Ernie; in any case it would have been no use intervening, Ernie only listened to those who agreed with him."[16]

The ministers most likely to have influenced the elaboration of foreign policy were those senior ministers who were members of the cabinet's Defence Committee (where any major discussions of foreign policy decisions took place before presentations to general Cabinet meeting), and those non-Cabinet Ministers of State who worked under Bevin at the Foreign Office. Consequently, in this study, attention will centre particularly on the following men who were the original members of Attlee's Defence Committee:

> A. V. Alexander (1945-46, 1st Lord of the Admiralty; 1946-50, Minister of Defence)
> C. R. Attlee   (Prime Minister)
> E. Bevin   (Foreign Secretary)
> R. S. Cripps   (1945-47, President of the Board of Trade; 1947-50, Chancellor of the Exchequer)
> E.H.J.N. Dalton (1945-47, Chancellor of the Exchequer)
> G. H. Hall   (1945-46, Secretary of State for the Colonies; 1946-51, First Lord of the Admiralty)
> J. J. Lawson   (1945-46, Secretary of State for War)
> H. Morrison   (Lord President of the Council)
> Lord Stansgate   (1945-46, Secretary of State for Air)
> J. Wilmot   (1945-47, Minister of Supply)

and on:

> H. MacNeill
> C. Mayhew
> P. J. Noel Baker

who worked with Bevin as Ministers of State at the Foreign Office.

No particular attention needs to be paid to members of the External Relations Committee, which was set up as a consultative parliamentary group for Bevin; he rarely attended its meetings and totally ignored its members' views. Attlee recorded in his memoirs that the group rarely met,[17] while Dalton in his memoirs gives an explanation of Bevin's alienation from the group; according to him it was composed of "pacifists and fellow travellers, pro-Russians and anti-Americans and every sort of freak harboured in our majority. . . the group as a whole was hopeless." Bevin, he went on to say, seldom met them, and the papers they prepared "if he ever read them merely infuriated him."[18]

From a study of the background of the thirteen men who were members of the Defence Committee or who worked with Bevin at the Foreign Office, it emerges that nine of them were brought up in middle-class homes, that eight of them attended private schools, (six of them Headmasters' Conference public schools), and that eight of them were university graduates. If one discounts Hall, Lawson, and Wilmot, who played least part in discussions and carried significantly less political muscle, the figures are even more revealing. Of the remaining ten, only two can be said to have come from working-class homes, and only three did not benefit from private school and university education. In terms of social background, therefore, the divide between leading cabinet members and leading Foreign Office officials was not enormous. In terms of age, there was a similar compatibility with the average age in 1945 of the former group being 56 and of the latter, 53.

The conservatism of the Foreign Office officials with regard to the foreign policy decision-making process was shared by the leading Cabinet Ministers. Whatever he might have implied in earlier years, when, for example, he had spoken of striking a "fatal blow" to the establishment the moment a Labour government took power, Attlee came to the Prime Minister's office believing that the government institutions he had inherited had had an inspired growth and that they should serve as models to the world.[19] The tone of his address to the Scottish T.U.C. in 1947 was typical: "We are rightly proud of our civil service which is second to none in the world for devotion to duty and for efficiency."[20] Bevin held similar views. Any distrust he may have felt for the civil service cadres and the traditional structure of government had disappeared during the war, when he had managed to work so harmoniously with his first Permanent Under-Secretary, Tom Phillips, and other officials at the Ministry of Labour and National Service. It was Bevin, in fact, who had to deal with those who criticized the existing process of foreign policy formulation. The controversy came to a head at the 1946 Labour Party conference, and he put up a formidable defence both of his staff and of their working methods. It was not merely inertia that made Bevin reject change but a positive approval of the system as it then existed. For example, on his return to London after the Paris Peace Conference, he told the cabinet

> he would like to put on record his appreciation of the part
> played by members of the Foreign Office staff. . . he had been
> especially impressed by the skill shown by the officials who
> had represented His Majesty's Government in the work of the
> various sub-commissions.[21]

Alexander, Cripps, Dalton, and Morrison often referred to the way in which British institutions were an example to the world, and there is no evidence that other members of the Defence Committee felt any differently.

The cabinet's admiration for the Foreign Office staff was reciprocated. It is true that, on occasion, Foreign Office officials made rather scathing remarks about the cabinet, but the remarks reflected the traditional civil service distrust of politicians rather more than any anti-Labour Party bias. Certainly the original fears of Orme Sargent (Permanent Secretary from 1946 to 1949) that the advent of a Labour government would lead to internal revolution and a weak foreign policy were soon dissipated, and there is no evidence that the Foreign Office staff gave the Attlee government any less respect than they had given to previous Tory and coalition administrations. Bevin, in particular, proved to be one of the most respected of all Foreign Secretaries. The mutual respect between Foreign Office and Cabinet was strengthened by the almost universal belief that British victory in war had vindicated the British system of government. For the Labour Cabinet, the situation was clear; the machine that had snatched Britain from the jaws of defeat and turned her into a conqueror could henceforth be used to bring about the changes in living conditions that were the party's major objectives.

In ideological outlook, the political leaders generally shared the empirical approach of the senior staff of the Foreign Office. The empirical approach is in reality the reflection of a certain ideological stance; it reflects a deep-seated contentment with the status quo and a motivation to maintain it, or at least only to modify it, in the face of very strong pressure. The empiricism of the senior Foreign Office officials evolved not so much from their reading of Burke as from their satisfaction at the world power position Britain had possessed since the end of the Napoleonic Wars. They were, in fact, motivated to preserve Britain's position intact and to make small piecemeal improvements as the opportunity arose. Empiricism is a conservative ideology and, strictly, would be incompatible with a socialist ideology, the objective of which is to change fundamentally and rapidly the existing order of things.

At first view, it would seem that the leading ministers in the Attlee Government approached affairs of state in a socialist rather than in an empirical frame of mind, for on the domestic front, at least, they came to office determined to change the existing order of society. The home economy was to be changed deliberately from one based primarily on the free play of market forces to one based much more on state control. The state was also to take on greater responsibility for the wellbeing of economically underprivileged groups and to effect measures that would lead to a more even distribution of resources among the population. However, it could be argued that the Attlee government's reform programme was merely an accommodation to pressures that threatened the status quo. Certainly most of the major reforms were the fulfillment of plans drawn up in the 1930s and planned in detail by various, often nonpolitical committees during the course of the war. Even if the Conservatives had been returned to power in 1945, a good number of these "socialist" reforms would probably still have taken place.

This said, it is certain that Cabinet leaders were motivated by something more than a mere desire to accommodate pressures that were strengthening the status quo. The pressures were there, but the Cabinet ministers themselves had been in part responsible for their existence and certainly gave them added impetus during their period in power. The decision to nationalize the steel and road transport industries is perhaps the best example of the role of socialist ideology in determining government actions during that period.

In the field of foreign policy, the situation was different; Cabinet members' thinking on foreign affairs reflected far less socialist ideology than it did the kind of empiricism traditionally associated with the Foreign Office. Bevin epitomized the empirical and functionalist approach. He did not believe in revolutionary change and profoundly distrusted the "talking shop" on international relations engaged in by the European continental states. As a former union negotiator, he much preferred advancing slowly, reaching a succession of small agreements, the cumulative effect of which would make progress towards the major aims of his policy. A classical example of his thought is contained in a wartime memorandum dealing with the postwar settlement:

> We must aim at an organization which will develop to the full such international services as transport and communications; which will encourage customs unions and develop international banking and lending facilities. It is such means as this that will guarantee the necessary cohesive force between nations while leaving political independence and theories of sovereignty untouched.[22]

In a Cabinet meeting in 1946 he criticized the French, who would not consider "building up their international position by a series of agreements on smaller issues," but who insisted on "raising major questions which were not yet ripe for international discussions."[23] Bevin once summarized his philosophy to his private secretary Barclay in these terms: "I am not a very strong believer in constitutions. I like the thing that grows, the thing that evolves."[24]

A COMPARISON OF ATTITUDES

Before concluding this chapter, it would be useful to move the focus away from structure and ideology to a comparison of the general attitudes held by both Cabinet members and Foreign Office officials with regard to Britain and her role in world affairs.

Among Cabinet members there was general agreement that Britain was a great world power with an unchallengeable role as a member of "the big three." At Potsdam, Dixon, Bevin's principal private secretary, noted in his diary:

> Bevin very effective at the meeting, with perhaps too pronounced slant towards Russia and against America, and a wholly delightful assumption that, of the three, we were still the biggest.[25]

Three years later, Bevin confided to Dalton, "If we only pushed on and developed Africa, we could have U.S. dependent on us, and eating out of our hand, in 4 or 5 years."[26]

Attlee's views were similar. In an expression of his foreign policy views made in 1944, he stated that Britain should play an equal part with the United States and Russia in the future world organization,[27] and in his speeches and letters after the victory had been won, he repeated the sentiment on many occasions, often making explicit his view that Britain should continue to lead the world as she had led it in the past.[28] Identical views were expressed by Alexander[29] and Morrison.[30] Even those with a reputation as socialist intellectuals had similar beliefs. Cripps, for example, said in an election address: "Our country and our Commonwealth must be powerful and strong because we want to be able to give leadership to the world towards greater peace and prosperity."[31] Attitudes such as these were, in fact, shared by most of the Labour left.[32] Indeed, the patriotism of English socialists had long been scorned by continental Marxists.[33]

The Cabinet's perception of Britain's world power status was shared by the staff of the Foreign Office. Cadogan, Bevin's first permanent secretary, in a letter to his wife from the San Francisco Conference, made it clear that he considered Britain to be an undisputed member of the big four world powers; other countries he dismissed as the "little fellows yapping at our heels."[34] Orme Sargent, who was to follow him in office, told Dixon two months later that he was very concerned that the Labour victory at the poll would mean that Britain would be reduced to a second-rank power.[35] It is thus not surprising that reactions against any suggestion of Britain losing her first-rate status appear frequently in the Foreign Office archives of the period.[36] Certainly the new power of the United States and Russia could not be ignored, but as one official commented,

> It would be a great mistake on our part to allow our sense of the power of the United States and Russia to prevent us from emphasizing the greatness of our people or the power of our Empire, both absolutely and comparatively.[37]

The view of Britain that prevailed in the Foreign Office is well summarized in a paper prepared by the Information Office of the British Embassy in Washington in 1945, which set out a general line to be followed by British officials in the United States. The paper advises officials to speak with authority and firmness and to recall to Americans ("this galvanic nation" whose new power "has somewhat gone to their heads"):

> (a) that in peace as in war we are able, tough, determined and dependable;

> (b) that the British Commonwealth and Empire will continue to be an essential world-wide system of strength and stability in a confused world;

> (c) that we will overcome the severe but temporary difficulties resulting from our war sacrifices, and rebuild our leadership in production and world trade;

> (d) that we are determined to set an example to the world in political democracy, individual freedom and social progress.

The paper concludes by reminding officials that "Britain is not a small island, but is the centre of a world-wide system with vital bases, great resources and extensive trade connections and goodwill." Moreover, the British Commonwealth "is the outstanding example of successful cooperation between free democracies." Grant McKenzie, who had prepared the paper, sent a copy to Attlee with a cover note explaining his conviction that it was necessary to prove "that we are strong as a nation and as the centre of a great progressive Commonwealth and Empire, and that, as a part of that strength we are becoming the moral and progressive leaders of the world."[38] This one paper draws together views about Britain that are found frequently in the comments of contemporary Foreign Office officials.

The views of the Cabinet and the Foreign Office officials coincided not only at a cognitive level but also very much at an affective level. Typical members of the Foreign Office had been to a public school at which the inculcation of patriotism would have been a major objective. They would then have pursued a career, the major raison d'etre of which would have been to defend and promote British interests. It is therefore not surprising to find evidence in official documents of their patriotism and love of country.

Bevin, though coming from a much different background, shared the same love of his country. He went out of his way to show that people from his background could love their country as intently as those of more gentle birth.

The following passage drawn from his speaking notes for the 1945 General Election campaign, illustrates his fierce patriotism:

> Perhaps the most outrageous claim of the Tory Party is that they alone love their country and are proud of the great free democracies making up the British Commonwealth. . . It is humbug and hypocrisy which no trade unionist can tolerate. The Labour Party will give place to no party in its loyalty and love of country.[39]

Gladwyn recalled that Bevin was "patriotic in the best sense of the word, that is to say that, without in any way being contemptuous of foreigners, he was proud to be English and always keen to establish and to fortify the place of our country in the world."[40]

In conclusion, Foreign Office officials and Cabinet ministers were of the same generation and came from similar social backgrounds. Both groups approached their work with the same empirical philosophy and believed that the value of traditional working methods had been well proved by the great victory over the Axis powers. They were also united by feelings of patriotism and a firm assurance that Britain should maintain her preeminent world position as the linking point between three "circles" or major power blocs: the United States, Russia and its dependencies, and the British Empire.

NOTES

1. Even Palmerston, of course, did not have a completely free hand. However, he certainly worked under fewer constraints than did his counterparts of the second half of the twentieth century. For analyses of foreign policy making in contemporary Britain, see Vital (1968) and Wallace (1976).

2. For a similar view, see Barber (1975) p. 276.

3. In British terminology a *public school* is one of a group of exclusive private schools loosely linked during the period under study by affiliation to the Headmasters' Conference, a forum for discussion of items of current interest. "Oxbridge" is an amalgam of Oxford and Cambridge universities, the two most prestigious British universities attended primarily by expublic school students.

4. Strang (1955) p. 70. During this period, most working men made less than £100 per annum; some made less than £50.

5. Kelly (1953) p. 9.

6. Sir Victor Mallet, Memoirs, (Unpublished at Churchill College, Cambridge) p. 1.

7. Rose (1959) p. 379.

8. Connell (1958) p. 278.

9. Ashton-Gwatkin (1949) p. 48. (My emphasis).

10. PRO, FO/317/44559, AN/239/23/45.

11. Strang (1955).

12. Young (1962) p. 49.

13. Lapie (1971) p. 56.

14. Strang (1956) p. 304.

15. A point confirmed by Sir Nicholas Henderson, Assistant Private Secretary to Bevin, 1945-47, in an interview with the author (29 May 1980).

16. Lord Shinwell, interview with the author, (17 June 1946).

17. Attlee Archives, Memoirs, p. 12.

18. Dalton (1962) p. 23.

19. Quoted in Addison (1975) p. 48. Cowling (1975) demonstrates well the difference in tone between Attlee's speeches when the Labour Party was in the wilderness in the 1930s and when it had prospects of victory in the general election at the end of the war.

20. Attlee Papers, Speech to Scottish T.U.C., 25 April 1947.

21. PRO, CM (46) 87 (17 October 1946).

22. Quoted in Bullock (1967) p. 205.

23. PRO, CM (46) 1st (1 January 1946) CAB 128/7

24. Barclay (1975) p. 67.

25. Dixon (1968) p. 170.

26. Dalton Diary, 15 October 1948.

27. PRO, CAB 66/53, WP 44/414, "Foreign Policy and the Flying Bomb," 26 July 1944.

28. See, for example, Attlee papers: speeches at National Union of Manufacturers (14 November 1946), Haileybury School (28 June 1946), and at the Lord Mayor's Banquet (9 November 1946).

29. See, for example, Alexander Papers: Derby War Memorial speech (27 September 1947) and LL. D. Investiture speech (1 July 1947).

30. Donoughue and Jones (1973) p. 510.

31. Cripps Papers, Election Broadcast, 20 June 1945.

32. See, for example, the views of Richard Crossman, one of the principal critics of Bevin's foreign policy and a leader of the parliamentary revolt of 1946 in Crossman (1946) p. 9.

33. Shils (1945) p. 511.

34. Dilks (1971) p. 746.

35. Dixon (1968) p. 166.

36. See, for example, PRO: FO 371/44535, AN/649/4/45 and FO 371/47858, N16807/18/38. Scc also Gladwyn (1972) p. 117.

37. PRO, FO/371/47450, N17623/10928/G63, F. Shepherd.

38. Attlee Papers, Correspondence with G. McKenzie, January 1946.

39. Bevin Papers, File 2/14.

40. Gladwyn (1972) p. 176.

4

Bevin's Relations With His Officials

The principal point of contact between Foreign Office and Cabinet was provided by the regular consultations held between Bevin and his leading officials. The nature of this relationship has been perceived in two clearly different ways. Many, particularly those of the political left, believed that Bevin, like Lord Grey before 1914, was dominated by Foreign Office officials; for others, it was Bevin who, like Lord Palmerston, provided some of the firmest leadership that the Foreign Office had ever experienced.

Bevin quickly came under fire from the political left, many of whom had hoped that the arrival at the Foreign Office of a Labour Foreign Secretary would herald radical changes in staffing and policy. In October 1945, Harold Laski, chairman of the Labour Party and among the most vociferous of the left-wing intellectuals, wrote about Bevin in a letter to Felix Frankfurter:

> Just because he is a "tough," people think he knows his own
> mind   The real truth is that he can be fooled with fantastic
> ease by the professionals who capture him with tales of how
> his wisdom is appreciated by the man on the spot.[1]

During the same period, Konni Zilliacus, one of the most vocal of the parliamentary Labour left, accused Bevin of trying to act out the role of Lord Palmerston wearing Keir Hardie's cloth cap, "whereas he was really the Foreign Office's Charley McCarthy."[2] This criticism was by no means confined to the left. Dalton, for example, quotes with approval an opinion expressed to him by Bruce Lockhart in autumn 1945:

> After only two months indoctrination, Bevin had become more
> devoted than any of his predecessors for a generation to the
> career diplomat and all the old boys in the Foreign Office, so

that very soon all the old nags were going back to the old
stables, "even Basil Newton."[3]

Criticism of Bevin increased throughout 1946. Many articles in the *New
Statesman* claimed that he was being dominated by the Foreign Office
professionals, and several similar accusations were made at the 1946 Labour
Party conference.[4]   Criticism of Bevin certainly eased after 1948 as socialist
admiration for the Soviet Union waned, but, nevertheless, accusations that the
Foreign Office imposed its way of thinking on him still persisted.
        There is a certain amount of evidence to lend credence to these
accusations. In his memoirs, Lord Gladwyn recounted his first meeting at the
Foreign Office with Bevin, who,

> said nothing for a few moments. . . and simply looked me over
> in my chair. Finally he observed, "must be kinda queer for a
> chap like you to see a chap like me sitting in a chair like this
> ... ain't never 'appened before in 'istory.". . . "Secretary of
> State," I said. . . "I am sorry that the first time I open my
> mouth in your presence is to contradict you. But you're
> wrong. . . a long time ago. . . there was then a butcher's boy
> in Ipswich whose origins, I suspect, were just as humble as
> your own, and he became Foreign Secretary of one of our
> greatest kings. . . His name was Tom Wolsey. And,
> incidentally, now I come to think of it, he was not unlike you
> physically." "Well," said the Secretary of State, visibly
> impressed, "I must say I never thought of that." From that
> moment onward I could do little wrong so far as Bevin was
> concerned.[5]

This recollection would seem to bear out the criticisms noted above. Bevin's
initial sense of independence from the Foreign Office establishment is broken
down by the judicious flattery of an official, whose real attitudes towards Bevin
must in some way be reflected in his reference to "Poor Uncle Ernie" later in the
paragraph. The same rather patronizing language is often used in the writings
of other Foreign Office officials.
        The need perceived by the Foreign Office officials to impose their ideas
on Bevin emerges clearly from the diaries of Sir Alexander Cadogan, who was
then the most senior Foreign Office official. Cadogan was appalled at the 1945
election results, but took some comfort that Bevin would become the new
Foreign Secretary. In his opinion, Bevin was better than "any of the other
Labourites."[6] The future could go reasonably well, Cadogan thought "if he,
Bevin, can be put on the right line." It is evident that Bevin very early accepted

or shared that Foreign Office line, for two weeks later Cadogan wrote, "talk with Bevin about his speech on foreign policy. He's got sound ideas which we must encourage."[7] By admitting his attempts to put Bevin "on the right line" and to "encourage" those ideas that the Foreign Office considered sound, Cadogan clearly demonstrates the collective will of the Foreign Office officials to impress their ideas and attitudes upon the new Secretary of State. Apparently their efforts were successful. Bevin, from the outset, relied much more on the advice of his Foreign Office advisers than he did on that of his political associates,[8] and he wholeheartedly defended the former group whenever they came under attack from the latter.[9]

A comment of Roderick Barclay, who served as a private secretary to Bevin, would seem to confirm that Bevin's ideas had to pass through several Foreign Office filters before they were put into effect. Writing of his regular morning meetings with Bevin, he remembered being

> ready with one or two enquiries about the significance of some comment or the reasons for his dissent from some recommendation. Having heard what was troubling him I could sometimes resolve the difficulty, or if not I could elucidate his views or interpret his instructions for the benefit of those directly concerned.[10]

According to another private secretary, Sir Nicholas Henderson, Bevin disliked drafting and relied on his officials to put his ideas and wishes into written form.[11] The filtering process was also referred to by yet another private secretary, Piers Dixon, who, while accompanying Bevin in the United States in winter 1946, wrote in his diary that he and Nicko (Nicholas Henderson) read the incoming telegrams and "passed on the tit-bits to EB."[12] There were instances of Bevin's being made to change his opinions on a course of action as a result of pressure from his officials at the Foreign Office; for example, in October 1945, Piers Dixon recalled how he had successfully discouraged Bevin from including in his statement a reference to Russian ambitions in the Mediterranean as a cause for the breakdown of the Peace Conference.[13]

In contrast, however, the records also reveal many instances that could serve to demonstrate Bevin's independence from his officials. The following excerpts from Dixon's diary are typical: "S of S made or issued 3 statements on Poland, Greece and admission of women to the foreign service. He disliked all 3 drafts sent up by the depts. and decided to rewrite them."[14] And a few weeks later: "Nicko and I altered E. B.'s speech. He refused most of the changes."[15]

Certainly to many foreign observers Bevin gave the air of being fully in control. The U.S. Secretary of State, James Byrnes, was so taken aback by his independence and aggression at Potsdam that he wondered how he would be able to get along with him. At the Potsdam Conference, Bevin did on occasion stamp his authority on his officials. Cadogan had advised Bevin to compromise on points of difference with the Russians, but his advice was ignored, and Bevin tried to increase demands on Russia and initiated some sharp exchanges with the Lublin Poles about the freedom and timing of elections. Ivonne Kirkpatrick, a senior Foreign Office official in Germany immediately after the war, recalled how at the peace conference, experts would send Bevin notes giving him material for his next intervention. Bevin apparently disagreed with many of these notes and tore them to pieces over his ashtray. As Kirkpatrick recorded, Bevin had great respect for many Foreign Office officials but could not be "bounced into doing anything against his better judgment."[16]   Barclay wrote that Bevin "treated [the Foreign Office staff]. . . as a benevolent uncle might treat some promising nephew, who had talent but still a good deal to learn about the ways of the world."[17]

In evaluating the relationship between Bevin and the Foreign Office staff, it is interesting to note how, despite the differences in social background, they shared a very similar ideological outlook. Kirkpatrick recalled:

> During our journeys I had many interesting talks with him on every conceivable subject: blood sports, the difficulty of running a socialist state without incentive, religion, the public schools, his Cabinet colleagues, the outlook of a docker. . . in general his outlook was robust and British; and one could foretell exactly what it would be in any given circumstance. He was a rock.[18]

Barclay recalled that many conservatives were surprised to see Bevin appear as a "cross between St. George and John Bull."[19] Bevin was at one with the Foreign Office in wishing to steer clear of appeasement through the adoption of franker and more assertive policies.[20]

Given this identity of outlook, it is difficult to talk of one party leading the other--both wished to travel in the same direction. In any event, the relationship could not be of a simple leader-follower type. If one had to give a direct answer to the question who was most influential in the foreign policy-making process, however, on balance, the answer would have to be the officials of the Foreign Office. In looking more closely at the instances in which Bevin disagrees with his staff, it is evident that the disagreement occurred generally at an action-tendency level only; for example, when Bevin stepped up Cadogan's proposed demands on Russia. At a cognitive and affective level, he and Cadogan were in complete agreement. Bevin may have introduced some changes of technique (and very few at that), but his attitudes at a cognitive and affective level drew heavily on what he learned from his staff.

One reason for this can be found, perhaps surprisingly, in an understanding of Bevin's trade union background. Bevin had always maintained his concern for the lot of the working man, but as his career as a union official had progressed, the improvement of union organization, which had been a means to that end, had become an end in itself. For many years before starting his political career, Bevin had spent most of his waking hours involved in union activities. He had very few other interests; his life was his work, and this influenced his approach to the Foreign Secretary's job. He consciously used his experience of negotiation within the trade union movement to assist him in his negotiations as Foreign Secretary, and often spoke of his work using trade union imagery.[21] For example, when Dalton, in October 1945, enquired how things were progressing at the Council of Foreign Ministers, Bevin replied, "like the strike leader said, 'thank God there is no danger of a settlement.'"[22] Indeed, Bevin saw himself as leader of the Foreign Office staff in the same way as he had seen himself as leader of the Transport and General Workers' Union. This meant defending the staff's position and fighting to improve its status. One Foreign Office official, Victor Mallet, described how Bevin firmly supported his career men, winning in the process their unstinted loyalty.[23] When criticism of the elite public school image of Foreign Office officials became fierce in 1946, Bevin rose to their defence in his old pugnacious style. He told the Cabinet flatly that he would not consider making the sweeping changes that his critics desired and merely promised to take steps "to strengthen the staff as opportunities arose."[24]

There was no doubt that Bevin felt a great sense of fraternity with his officials, and after difficult sessions of one of the peace conferences, he would at times "assemble his devoted staff in his suite after dinner and. . . lead them in old fashioned (but perfectly decorous) choruses."[25] When his health forced him finally to give up his position as Secretary of State, he told a former colleague at the Foreign Office, Sir William Strang, how much he felt a part of the Foreign Office team. Talking of the staff, he wrote, "All have been a joy. . . I am very proud of my colleagues who had faced with me all these great decisions on policy."[26] Bevin saw himself as the representative of the Foreign Office staff. There was no doubt that he fought to defend its rights and its reputation. In view of these facts, it could be expected that he would fight also to defend its ideas.

Bevin's ill health provides a second reason why he would have been likely to have accepted the direction of his officials. After suffering a coronary thrombosis in 1946, he was plagued by increasingly severe attacks of angina in the following years. He was frequently in pain; his energy flagged; he would often doze at meetings; in general, he became less capable of the energetic and independent leadership for which he had won his reputation. Already by the second year of the government's life he was a very sick man. After the return from the summer recess in October 1946, Dalton recorded in his diary:

Most Ministers seemed better for the break, although E. B.
when I first met him on return, seemed to me pretty feeble,
with a very weak voice and a sense of being generally baffled.
On later occasions he has picked up a bit, but is still not at all
the man he was.[27]

Some four months later he wrote:

E. B. is in no fit condition to go on much longer. This
afternoon he was in a state of total exhaustion, as a result of
having to walk up 2 flights of steps at Great George St. Just
how he will fare at Moscow is anybody's guess. It is quite on
the cards, I fear, that he may not come back. . . he has a
doctor always with him.[28]

Bevin's health was in fact so bad that his physician, Sir Alec McCall,
once remarked that the only sound thing about him was his feet.[29]   Bevin was
kept going by numerous injections--he once introduced McCall by saying, "this
is Alec, he treats my behind like a dartboard"--and pills or the so-called pellets
that his detective Ben Massey carried constantly. He was also helped in no small
measure by the efforts of his private office in planning his itineraries to avoid
stairs and undue physical exertion and in making not always successful attempts
at cutting down his consumption of alcohol.[30]
        The diaries of Pierson Dixon contain constant references to Bevin's ill
health and how frequently he would become worn down by pain and fatigue.[31]
Incidentally, Dixon also felt that Mrs. Bevin reduced her husband's ability to
concentrate on his work. In one uncharacteristically bitter entry, he wrote:

If Mother B. nagged at him, he talked about being drawn to
resign and was bloody-minded about the treaty negotiations. .
. an impossible woman with the mind of a louse, the traditions
of a working-class woman and the airs of an Empress.[32]

According to his daughter Queenie, in summer 1946, Bevin was not only
physically ill but also "his nerves [were] absolutely in pieces."[33]
        In fairness, it should be pointed out that Bevin never completely lost his
grip. Barclay recalled that

Mr. Bevin's normal working week would have been enough to
exhaust a much younger and fitter man. This was not only
achieved as a result of sheer determination and at the cost of
considerable physical suffering, but he remained passionately

interested in the job and his grip on affairs never really weakened.[34]

Bevin never became a puppet, but it would be reasonable to assume that his tiredness and pain made him more prone, at least on certain occasions, to follow the line of least resistance and to accept the recommendations of his staff. His acceptance of their ideas was facilitated by the basic similarities of their world outlook.

There is another fundamental reason why Bevin was motivated to accept Foreign Office views. When Bevin became Secretary of State for Foreign Affairs, he realized that he had reached one of the pinnacles of the establishment. He was proud to be accepted by this group and, as could have been predicted, became inclined to adopt for himself the attitudes that he felt that group possessed. The insecurity that Bevin felt beneath his bluff exterior and his need to feel accepted by the group made him cling all the more tenaciously to their attitudes.

To understand Bevin's insecurity, one needs to remember his childhood experience. He was born illegitimate in Winisford, a small west country village, and was brought up in considerable poverty, first by his mother and subsequently by an older sister. During this period in the late nineteenth century neither his poverty nor his illegitimacy would have gone unstigmatized. On the rare occasions that Bevin spoke of his very early life, it was generally with some bitterness. Chuter-Ede, later to be one of his Cabinet colleagues, described a lunchtime meeting with Bevin that took place in March 1945, when Bevin strenuously supported arguments for the abolition of all payments in schools. "He did this," Chuter-Ede wrote in his diary,

> because of the miseries of his boyhood. His mother died when
> he was 9 years old. His school pence were paid by the
> Guardians and, when the other boys walked out with their two
> pences and three pences, he sat in his place with half a dozen
> others.[35]

Bevin was, however, handicapped not only by his birth and poverty but also by his physical appearance; he was short and overweight and possessed a noticeable squint. When he tried to enlist for the Marines he was turned down because of his size, a decision that he resented.[36] Bevin sought with enormous energy to escape from the inferior status to which he had been assigned. He, at first, generalized his problem to the working classes as a whole. As his official biographer observed, "socialism to Bevin meant something more than planning and public ownership; it meant a change in the status of the worker, the end of that exclusion from responsibility, the stigma of inferiority."[37] He still saw things in these terms after moving into the political arena. The first benefit that came to his mind after the Labour Party's service in the War Cabinet was that it would have removed the inferiority complex among "our people."[38]

When Bevin reached the Foreign Office he had finally proved that he was not inferior. He had achieved a position of respect in society, something for which, at a subconscious level at least, he had been working all his life. The achievement of this goal gave him enormous satisfaction. He enjoyed musing on the journey he had made from insignificant country boy to world leader. Those who had rejected him would now have to alter their opinions. The feeling of compensation for early injustices was never far from his mind. He once exclaimed to one of his staff, "I have the DCL of Bristol. I have been elected fellow of Magdalen. And I left school when I was eleven!"[39] On leaving the Foreign Office he wrote to Strang, "I was born into a poor little home and went to a poor little school and look what I have done in the world. There must be some purpose in it." What his position had meant to him becomes forcefully apparent in the next phrase, "and now they want to throw me on the scrap heap."[40]

In an effort to establish himself, Bevin became, in some ways, more royal than the king. He was enthralled by reminiscences of the old Foreign Office and often asked questions such as, "What would Lord Curzon do if he were in my shoes?"[41] On one occasion, he even asked what Queen Elizabeth would have done.[42] Bevin in many ways felt closer to the traditional elite classes in British society than he did to members of his own Labour Party. He never ceased proclaiming his identity with the working classes, "my people," as he called them, but he saw himself as their leader and protector much more than as an ordinary member of their group. Certainly, his life-style moved further and further away from that of the working class. Gladwyn claims that Bevin once said to him,

> "You know Gladwyn, I don't *mind* the upper class. As a matter of fact I even rather like the upper class." (I think by "upper class," [Gladwyn explained], he meant anybody who had been to a good public school, not only Dukes or Earls.) "They may be an abuse but they are often, as like as not, intelligent and amusing. Of course I love the lower class. It's my class and it's the backbone of this country. But, Gladwyn, what I frankly can't abide is the middle class. For I find them self-righteous and narrow minded."[43]

Bevin had a very easy relationship with many Conservative MPs; he wrote affectionately to the right-wing Leopold Amery;[44] he liked Duff Cooper, a favorite target of the left, so much that he prolonged his stay as Ambassador in Paris;[45] he frequently, and of his own volition, consulted with Anthony Eden;

and his relationship with Winston Churchill was mostly warm and at times overwhelmingly sentimental.[46]   He developed an easy relationship with the Royal Family as well. Queen Mary was a sincere admirer and gave Bevin a personal key to Marlborough House Garden, and King George VI wrote in a letter to the Duke of Gloucester that although he found it difficult to talk with most of the members of the new Labour Government, "Bevin is very good and tells me everything that is going on. The others are still learning how to run their departments."[47]

He became a warm admirer of Eton and Harrow, the two public schools most generally associated with the education of the rich and privileged, and defended the public schools in general in speeches not only at Eton itself but also at Labour Party conferences. He relaxed with pleasure at private and exclusive London clubs such as the Garrick and the Atheneum. Dixon records one weekend spent on a yacht in the Solent and another at Windsor Castle where, rather scandalously, it seems he felt sufficiently self-assured to suggest a future, more private meeting to one of the ladies-in-waiting. Admittedly, however, this latter episode probably reflects nothing more than Bevin's sense of humour.

Bevin's relationship with the traditional elite groups contrasts greatly with his relations within the Labour Party. Dalton recalled that "Bevin knew very few [Labour MPS]. . . and made no serious efforts to extend his knowledge."[48]   Woodrow Wyatt, writing at a time when he had grown to admire Bevin, recalled that he was "a distant figure" not much in contact with the party.[49]

In short, while the view that Bevin was "captured" and "fooled" by the Foreign Office officials is both simplistic and incorrect, it is true that for a number of both psychological and practical reasons he was predisposed to bring his attitudes into line with theirs and to accept their advice.

NOTES

1. Martin (1953) p. 186.

2. Martin (1953) p. 185.

3. Dalton (1962) p. 104. Dalton, however, enjoyed making a spiteful remark; had he gone to the Foreign Office he would probably have treated the staff in a similar way.

4. See, for example, *New Statesman*, 10 August 1946.

5. Gladwyn (1972) pp. 175-176.

6. Dilks (1971) p. 776.

7. Dilks (1971) p. 778.

8. See, for example, Dixon (1968) p. 179.

9. See, for example, Labour Party Conference Report (1946) p. 164.

10. Barclay (1975) p. 37.

11. Interview with the author, 28 May 1980.

12. Dixon Diary, 13 November 1946.

13. Dixon Diary, 8 October 1945.

14. Dixon Diary, 20 March 1946.

15. Dixon Diary, 24 May 1946.   The speech was referring to the Egyptian problem.

16. Kirkpatrick (1959) p. 202.

17. Barclay (1975) pp. 46-47.

18. Kirkpatrick (1959) p. 204.

19. Barclay (1975) p. 82.

20. See below.

21. Barclay (1975) p. 88.

22. Dalton Diary, 5 October 1945.

23. Mallet Memoirs, p. ix.

24. PRO, CAB 128/7, CM (46) 14, 11 February 1946.

25. Gladwyn (1972) p. 189.

26. Strang (1956) p. 296.

27. Dalton Diary, 23 October 1946.

28. Dalton Diary, 6 February 1947.

29. Barclay (1975) pp. 46-47.

30. Barclay (1975) pp. 47-48, 65.

31. Dixon Diaries (4 March 1946, 12 July 1946, 30 July 1946, 7 August 1946, 8 August 1946, 7 February 1947).

32. Dixon Diary, 18 December 1946.

33. Dixon Diary, 30 July 1946.

34. Barclay (1975) p. 48.

35. Chuter-Ede Diaries, 29 March 1945.

36. Hollis (1956) p. 155.

37. Bullock (1960) p. 514.

38. From a letter to C. R. Attlee quoted in Bullock (1967) p. 381.

39. Dixon (1968) p. 214.

40. Strang (1956) p. 296.

41 Kirkpatrick (1959) p. 202.

42. Minney (1958) p. 92.

43. Gladwyn (1972) p. 177.

44. PRO, FO/371/50924, U9861/59821/70 (26 November 1945).

45. Barclay (1975) p. 60.

46. Pakenham (1953) p. 233.

47. Quoted in Wheeler-Bennett (1958) p. 652.

48. Dalton (1962) p. 23.

49. Wyatt (1952). Other works describing Bevin's relationship with the Labour Party include Gordon (1969), Rose (1959), Shaw (1974), and Windrich (1959).

Part 2

The Attitudes
of the Policymakers

5

Attitude Formation
in Childhood Years

In seeking to understand how British policymakers formed their attitudes with regard to Britain's role in the world, it is first necessary to consider the intellectual environment of their formative years around the turn of the century, when they would have first become aware of their national identity. It will be recalled that attitudes formed during a person's youth are likely to be the most potent and the most resistent to change.[1]

The quarter century preceding the First World War was a period of deeply held yet often conflicting emotions. At one level it was for Britain a period of pride and self-satisfaction marking the zenith of the country's power and worldwide influence; at another it was a period of concern at the country's economic and moral weakness.

At the first level, there was satisfaction at Britain's continuing world leadership in trade and financial matters and pride in the vast pink areas on world maps and globes that confirmed the imperial presence overseas. The Boer War, which broke out late in 1899, although not universally popular, was accompanied by a more fervent jingoism than had been apparent during the years of the Crimean War when that word had been coined.[2] British successes in muddling through this most undistinguished war often formed the subject of massive yet spontaneous public demonstrations. This patriotic fervour was reinforced by the music halls and other elements of popular culture, and also by the politicians as they went out to win votes from the new mass electorate.[3]

Britain's position in world affairs was no longer the subject of the kind of debate that had been so common in the mid-nineteenth century. Generally, the public had accepted the view that Britain's world empire and preeminent position in international affairs was the natural outcome of the course of British history. The prevailing view of history around the turn of the century was overwhelmingly Whig in its orientation; in other words it was characterized by:

> the belief that English institutions like no others in the Western world, were the result of slow growth from Saxon days; that, like a coral reef, precedent had fallen on precedent, erecting a bulwark of liberty, creating institutions such as Parliament or constitutional monarchy. Many centuries and much tribulation had been required to bring these to perfection; their antiquity, their slow growth endowed them with a special virtue, and British history therefore was a moral as well as political example to mankind.[4]

Macaulay, who exemplified the Whig approach to history and who was still widely read, characterized the British as:

> The greatest and most highly civilised people that ever the world saw. . . which have spread their dominion over every corner of the globe. . . which have carried the science of healing, the means of locomotion and correspondence, every mechanical art, every manufacture, everything that promotes the convenience of life, to a perfection which our ancestors would have thought magical; have produced a literature which may boast of works not inferior to the noblest which Greece has bequeathed to us; have discovered the laws which regulate the motions of the heavenly bodies, have speculated with exquisite subtlety on the operations of the human mind, have been the acknowledged leaders of the human race in the career of political improvement.[5]

The impact of such writings was all the stronger when associated with the concepts of social Darwinism that were prevalent around the turn of the century. Spencer's early writings that had argued that the "fittest" human beings would become the "select of their generation" had been applied far more widely than the author had first intended. For example, much was said and written during this period of living and dying nations, and for many the justification for British preeminence in world affairs could be found in the innate racial superiority of its inhabitants. As Cecil Rhodes, perhaps the most famous imperial administrator, is reported to have said, "We are the first race in the world and the more of the world we inherit, the better it is for the human race."[6] Many likened the British situation to that of Rome, an imperial power that had achieved more than any other before its long decline and decay.

However, although the Edwardian period was one of great optimism and self-satisfaction, pessimism was never far away. Early in the new century, Lord Curzon, one of Bevin's predecessors at the Foreign Office, wrote with some foreboding, "The pessimists are abroad in the land. We can hardly take up our morning newspaper without reading of the physical and moral decline of the race."[7] The historian Arthur Bryant recalled that "before the war it had become commonplace among elderly gentlemen of the military profession and others that England was going to the dogs and that its young men, clinging timorously to the office stool and the suburban villa, had lost the gallant spirit of their fathers."[8]

The malaise had been provoked by a number of factors. First, the potential power that could be wielded by Germany and the United States could no longer be overlooked. In economic terms, German production in many fields had already begun to outstrip that of Britain, and the overwhelming British predominance in world trade appeared inevitably to be at risk. The dangers were well publicized in a number of best-selling books during the 1890s.[9] Fuller employment after 1900 perhaps lessened the general concern, but it was of course still acutely felt by those involved in the creation of foreign and economic policy.

The revelations of the Boer War also contributed powerfully to the malaise. The poor physical condition of army recruits set up fears of the physical decline of the race and the poor soldiering and the difficulties encountered in subduing the ill-prepared, inexperienced and, in the eyes of some, a racially inferior group, raised questions about Britain's capacity to assert her will in the world in what was seen as the traditional manner.

The rise of working class political movements also gave grounds for concern. The socialists were calling for a share in political power and had demonstrated a seeming lack of patriotism in denouncing the Boer War. It was not clearly recognized at the time that their main objection to the war was that it detracted from the debate on social reform and not that the independence of the Boers was under attack. Among the workers themselves a desire for more social benefits did not prevent their participation in the spontaneous demonstrations that followed some of the key successes in the war campaign. However this may be, the rise of a new social class seemingly dedicated to radical change of the social structure, and hence the accepted manner of governing the country, could only be viewed with some trepidation by the generally conservative middle and upper classes that had been accustomed for so long to a monopoly of power.

Among the "pessimists" referred to by Lord Curzon could also perhaps be included a significant section of the Liberal Party that regularly expressed opposition to the "Caesarism" of the Tories, to the desire to expand abroad to "places where no white man can live" and to "false ideals of national greatness and national honour."[10] Although several radicals and "Little Englanders" were calling for a halt to further imperial expansion during this period, there is no evidence that any of them would have advocated the liquidation of the existing British Empire or presence overseas.[11]

During this period, public attitudes towards Britain at an affective level were characterized by a deep national pride; there was no questioning of the deserved preeminence of the British people either in terms of world power or in terms of national culture and experience. At a cognitive level, however, there was some dissonance, because intertwined with evidence of British preeminence was evidence that the country's position was being challenged and undermined.

Attempts to diminish this dissonance took many forms. In some cases the threats to the perception of British greatness were recognized objectively, and counteractions were taken; for example, the naval programme was expanded to ensure the continuation of British sea power under threat from Germany, and military reforms and some social benefits were inaugurated to deal with the problems that had become so painfully apparent during the Boer War. Often, however, the dissonance-reducing behaviour took less objective and less specific form. Many advanced the argument that since British preeminence had been won by the spiritual qualities of the British people, any threats to the country's position could best be repulsed by a vigorous reacceptance of those values that had weakened with the passage of time. Much energy was expended in extolling the merits of bravery, patriotism, loyalty, honesty, and all the virtues that were seen to have made Britain great in the past and which would be needed in the future if Britain were to resume her position of unchallenged greatness. Any evidence of the exercise of these virtues was hungrily seized upon. The last words of Captain Scott, who in 1912 had set out to reach the South Pole, employing British courage rather more than scientific planning, provide but one example of the widespread but deep desire to vindicate British superiority:

> I do not regret this journey, which has shown that Englishmen can endure hardships, help one another, and meet death with as great a fortitude as ever in the past. . . this enterprise, which is for the honour of our country. . . Had we lived I should have had a tale to tell of the hardihood, endurance and courage of my companions which would have stirred the heart of every Englishman. These rough notes and our dead bodies must tell the tale.[12]

The greatest efforts to build patriotism and a desire to preserve British preeminence were directed towards the youth, a fact clearly revealed by a study of the period's juvenile literature, youth movements, and schools.

Many writers of books for young people during this period approached their work with a definite and specific design to inspire patriotism and what were seen as traditional British virtues in their readers and thus contribute to the raising of a generation that would push aside the contemporary threats to Britain's world power position. For example, in *Us and Our Empire*, a book first published in 1911 and widely distributed, probably often as a school or Sunday school prize, the young hero is made to say:

> Our Empire will be on its last legs unless we do something. And we've got to do it. . . England is going down because she's losing her ideals. . . Long ago men did and dared from sheer love for their king and country. They kept high and noble things in front of them, and tried to act up to them. Now England isn't doing it, and whenever in history the nation isn't inspired by noble ideas, however big and rich they are, they simply go down and down, and waste away to nothing.

The child who made this analysis then proposes the solution:

> The whole world's eyes will be upon us to see if we're going to pull it up again. . . The grown-up men and women have made a hash of it. . . We're Britain's hope and we'll jolly well see we don't play her false. . . We must be proper patriots and love our mother country like nothing else--fight for her and die for her.[13]

The most popular books and magazines, those that children would have chosen for themselves, most frequently contained stories inspired by a highly biased and romanticized interpretation of British history. Kipling is the most obvious example of a writer who returned again and again in his books to a description of the greatness of England's world mission. G. A. Henty was more widely read by young people and specialized in historical stories that described some great English victories. The preface to *Clive in India* describes the structure of a typical Henty story:

> In the following pages I have endeavoured to give you a vivid picture of the wonderful events of the ten years, which at their commencement saw Madras in the hands of the French, Calcutta at the mercy of the Nabob of Bengal, and English influence apparently at the point of extinction in India, and which ended in the final triumph of the English both in Bengal and in Madras. There were yet great battles to be fought, great efforts to be made before the vast Empire of India fell altogether into British hands.[14]

Other great British victories were celebrated in a prolific list of titles ranging from *Under Drake's Flag* (1883) to *With Kitchener in the Soudan* (1903). Henty affected the outlook of a generation of boys. As Thornton concluded:

> His significance as a writer is nil; but the matter of the stories he told is part of the historical evolution of the sentiment of confident imperialism.[15]

Henty's work was typical of other reading material for boys. In a world before radio and television, books had a much greater influence. Thinking back to his school days, which had begun in Edwardian times, George Orwell explained:

> The books one reads in childhood, and perhaps most of all the bad and good bad books, create in one's mind a sort of false map of the world, a series of fabulous countries into which one can retreat at odd moments throughout the rest of life and which in some cases can even survive a visit to the real countries which they are supposed to represent.[16]

Youth clubs and movements on a national scale first came into being in the two decades preceding the First World War. What proportion of the youth of the time they touched is unclear, so their importance should not be overemphasized. It is worth noting, however, that their founders saw them as providing a means to defend the British Empire from moral and spiritual decline. As Baden-Powell wrote to his boy scouts:

> Remember whether rich or poor, from castle or from slum, you are all Britons in the first place, and you've got to keep Britain up against outside enemies, you have to stand shoulder to shoulder to do it. If you are divided among yourselves you are doing harm to your country.[17]

Similarly, William Smith founded the "Boys Brigade" as an organization in which boys could learn the value of both Christianity and national pride.[18] Indeed, all of the national youth movements of any significance in the pre-First World War period were imperialist and militarist in nature. It was not until the 1920s that movements with alternative ideological foundations emerged.[19]

More than from reading books and from participating in youth movements, the future policymakers would have learned attitudes from their schools. It was during the period under review that schools, and particularly the public schools, made the most conscious efforts to ensure that all students passing through their doors should leave as Christians, good sportsmen, patriots, and servants of the empire. As J. E. Welldon, Headmaster of Harrow, said in 1899:

> An English Headmaster, as he looks to the future of his pupils will not forget that they are destined to be the citizens of the greatest Empire under Heaven; he will teach them patriotism not only by his words but by his example. . . He will inspire them with faith in the divinely ordered mission of their country and their race; he will impress upon their young minds the convictions that the great principles upon which the happiness of England rests--the principles of truth, liberty, equality and religion--are the principles which they must carry into the world.[20]

Evidence of many types--school magazines, examination papers, speech day reports, memoirs--shows how closely the public schools followed these ideas.[21] Every effort was made to ensure that the teaching faculty believed in the teachings they were to give. It was, for example, not unknown for teachers seeking appointment in the public schools to be asked whether they saluted the Union Jack or stood bareheaded for the National Anthem.[22]

History teaching in the schools both public and state reflected, as could have been predicted, a heavy nationalistic bias. Overwhelming evidence for this was amassed by the Carnegie Foundation for International Peace that published in 1924 a study of history textbooks used by combatant countries during the Great War, and also by other international institutions that conducted similar studies during the same period.[23] One writer in a 1926 study showed how historical accounts of incidents such as the bombardment of Copenhagen or the Indian Mutiny were used to bolster patriotism rather than give cause for any reevaluation of British policy.[24] Some three years later another writer concluded from a study of school history textbooks, most of which were in use before 1914:

> The prevailing note of many history books is the Kipling attitude, which is still almost unchallenged in the tradition and teaching of the public schools. Imperialism in the widely read and well written stories of Mr. Rudyard Kipling is picturesque and powerfully attractive. The Anglo-Saxon, resourceful, fearless and undaunted, makes the road, builds the bridge, cleans out the fever swamp and rescues the disordered 'lesser breeds' from their petty hates and love of darkness. God's chosen people were the apostles of even-handed justice,

relentless veracity, personal cleanliness and modern efficiency.[25]

The image of Britain that was taught in the schools was not one of an industrial country competing with increasing difficulty against new emerging powers, but was rather one of the Great World power, the victor of wars against Louis XIV and Napoleon--most history then stopped at 1815--and the current head of a mighty empire. Britain was seen as the mother of democratic governments, the country that had progressed furthest towards the perfect state; a political and moral example to the world.

The concepts concerning Britons and the role of their country taught in the schools interlocked easily with the leisure-time reading that depicted valiant English heroes combatting the treacherous foreigner and with the ethos of the Boy Scouts and other youth movements. There can be no doubt that the children and youth of the epoch were subjected to a strong process of indoctrination; this fact cannot by itself, however, prove that they accepted for themselves the attitudes that their elders were trying so hard to inculcate within them. It is without doubt easier to describe how political and other ideas were propagated than how they were received by their audience. Fortunately, several of Attlee's Cabinet members and several Foreign Office leaders have preserved their recollections of childhood and the attitudes they formed at that time.

Clement Attlee came from a solid middle class home. His father was a Gladstonian Liberal, but his brother Bernard was strongly Conservative and more influential on the young Attlee's thinking.[26] Attlee remembered that his school days coincided with a "most reactionary period," which he described as the high tide of "imperialism." His school, Haileybury, originally the school for those going to the India Company and later to the Indian Civil Service, he remembered, "was at that time extremely jingoist."[27] Attlee himself was caned after he and his friends had celebrated the relief of Ladysmith during the Boer War with a raucous victory march through the streets of Hertford and Ware. Many years later Attlee explained how his attitudes towards Britain's world role were influenced by the teachings at Haileybury:

> On the wall at school hung a great map with large portions of it coloured red. It was an intoxicating vision for a small boy, for, as we understood it, all these people were ruled for their own good by strong, silent men, civil servants and soldiers as portrayed by Kipling. We believed in our great Imperial mission.[28]

After Haileybury, Attlee went on to Oxford where he read history under the Whig historians Arthur Johnson and Ernest Barker. Speaking of this period in his memoirs, he wrote:

> I was myself a Protectionist and a Tory, a legacy from
> Haileybury. . . The country was still under the spell of the
> Imperialism which Kipling preached and which was so much
> strengthened by the pomp and circumstance of the Diamond
> Jubilee and the Jingoism of the South African War.[29]

Attlee's colleagues who attended public schools shared this intellectual heritage and, interestingly, many of them were active Tories.

In 1910, the young Stafford Cripps campaigned energetically for his father, a Conservative candidate for election to Parliament.   Dalton, who, incidentally, had spent much of his childhood in Windsor where his father was chaplain to the Royal Family, recalled:

> I was against the Liberals. I was a Joe Chamberlainite, a Tory
> Democrat, a self-confessed Imperialist. I gave a big book
> about the Empire to Kindersley when I left. He was a Liberal
> free trader and I wanted to educate him.[30]

Those Cabinet Ministers who attended state schools seem to have been influenced in similar ways. Morrison, for example, was born into an upper working class, staunchly conservative home. He was an avid reader of comic papers and boys stories and frequented the music hall--in many instances during this period a propagator of patriotic values[31]--as often as funds would allow. He enjoyed learning English history through the pages of Macaulay and Green.[32] Alexander recalled Kipling and Henty as among his favorite childhood authors. Emmanuel Shinwell, another Labour minister, recalled how, at the time of the Boer War, he had been "a fervid Tory, ready and willing to go to Africa and fight Kruger with my bare hands."[33]

Very little is known of the details of Bevin's early life. The record books of the schools he attended give more details of weather and absences than they do of subjects taught and textbooks used.[34] However, there is no reason to believe that the intellectual climate in his schools was any different from those of his Cabinet colleagues. It is known that Bevin was brought up as an active member of an evangelical Methodist Church group. At chapel he would undoubtedly have heard accounts of how brave English missionaries were taking the gospel and civilization to people in foreign lands. On leaving school and home he acquired a taste for the music hall, from which he memorized a large number of popular refrains. So while, Bevin, unlike Attlee and other senior colleagues, never commented specifically on how school, church, and popular culture had influenced the formation of his early attitudes towards Britain, it is reasonable to say that the balance of evidence indicates that their influence was probably broadly similar. It is noteworthy that in none of his surviving writings or speeches can there be found any questioning of the fundamental correctness of Britain's world power status; in fact, he held in scorn socialist intellectuals and any who questioned Britain's imperial role.

Memories of their childhood concepts of Britain and her world role were very similar among leading members of the Foreign Office. Sir William Strang recalled:

> Soon after I had learned to read, I came upon a little red-covered world geography. I was fascinated by the maps. I was made intensely proud by the amount of red that appeared on them. I anxiously compared the figures for commerce and industry of the United Kingdom with those of her rivals, and since my little book was twenty years out of date, the story told by these figures was a triumphant one. I was saddened by cartoons which I sometimes saw, suggesting that this preeminence might be threatened. I was aghast at one of them which showed a ragged and emaciated John Bull pushing a poorly supplied barrow and an opulent Uncle Sam remarking, "And to think that when I first knew the man he was rich and prosperous."[35]

It will be recalled that Lord Franks's vision of his childhood atlas was similarly intoxicating.

Gladwyn had the following memories of his period at prep school:

> I need hardly say that the general atmosphere was immensely conservative. In the 1910 election we spent much time sticking little blue stamps on the "Observer" map of Great Britain. . . and when the preponderant Liberal and Radical red was much diminished there was great rejoicing. . . It was, after all, the heyday of the British Empire and we were imperialists almost to a boy.[36]

Sir David Kelly recalled the pressures on public school boys to conform to the constellation of generally accepted attitudes. He described what he called the cult of the public school spirit, in these terms:

> In the early years of the twentieth century, the cult had reached a point of religious intensity and had crystallized into a fetish worship. The public schoolboy's code and the public schoolmaster's attitude, had become a sacred body of custom similar to that of a savage tribe; and the slightest deviation in voice, manner, clothes or ideas was sufficient to ensure a boycott.[37]

Members of Attlee's Cabinet and the leaders of the Foreign Office grew up during the heyday of British imperialism and formed similar attitudes concerning their country's world role. As will be seen later these early attitudes were to prove quite resistant to change. Just as Attlee was openly called an Edwardian figure during the 1940s, so was Orme Sargent, the most senior member of the Foreign Office staff during most of the period under study. Sir John Wheeler Bennet knew Sargent well and described him as "a survival of a past age, almost an anachronism. In appearance, tradition, conventions, standards and values, he was essentially Edwardian with all the elegance and elan of that period."[38]

Although obviously many of the attitudes first adopted by the political and Foreign Office leaders were modified during the course of time, those attitudes concerning Britain and her world role appear to have been least subject to modification. In the late 1940s these leaders still took it for granted that Britain was the most politically advanced and sophisticated nation, that she could teach others but had nothing to learn from them, and that her world empire and the collective wisdom of her leaders entitled her to a voice in world affairs that would be second to none. Some members of the Attlee Government modified their childhood attitudes as they found that the realities of poverty and unequal income distribution were irreconcilable with their early classical Liberal or Tory views. Attlee was converted to socialism by working with the poor in the East end of London. His colleague, Herbert Morrison, who grew up among the poor of that same city, was converted to socialism by listening to street-corner preachers and observing the conditions of the poor people in his neighbourhood. There is no evidence, however, that this change in their political views and economic views was accompanied by change in their views of the great power status of their country. Both Attlee and Morrison, like others in the Cabinet, dedicated most of their energies to improving and changing the internal status quo and devoted considerably less attention to foreign affairs.

The career of Herbert Morrison provides an interesting case study. His biographers noted that around the time of his political awakening, "Foreign affairs he paid scant attention to; his focus was on domestic issues."[39] He did object strongly to the First World War, but his view of England's role in the world was little affected. In 1921, as Mayor of Hackney, he disagreed with party colleagues and gave special orders that Union Jacks were to be flown from all municipal buildings during the visit of the Prince of Wales.[40] He entered Parliament in the mid-1920s where, compared with his contributions on domestic issues, his interventions on foreign issues were sparse and showed no signs of original thinking or wide reading.[41] During the 1930s he made several trips abroad. Far from creating dissonance these trips reinforced earlier views. On returning from one trip he said, "I hope I am not a Jingo, but I feel that perhaps the British are the most considerate colonial administrators of any government in the world."[42] Returning from another, he said, "I'm glad to be back. When

I saw England again, I thought what a wonderful country it is. There is something so sound about it all."[43]

His overall approach to foreign affairs remained unchanged throughout the 1930s. He formed his views of foreign policy without the detailed analysis he gave to home politics, tending to accept the conventional line of the party, which, according to his biographers, fitted neatly into the set of attitudes he had acquired before 1914.[44] His approach remained the same after the war. In 1947, Lapie, a leading French bureaucrat, shuddered at "l'homme bourru et insulaire qui est Morrison."[45] He became increasingly nostalgic as the 1940s drew to a close and his thinking seemed more powerfully influenced by his early Edwardian attitudes. These attitudes had always been strong, but by 1951 when he replaced Bevin at the Foreign Office, his biographers remarked that he had grown a little more jingoistic, more blimpish, and less tolerant.[46] On his arrival at the Foreign Office, he asked for a life of Palmerston which he ostentatiously carried around with him for several weeks.[47]

The pattern of Morrison's thinking over the years was matched in the lives of most of his Cabinet colleagues. For example, on arriving at the Treasury, Dalton sought out biographies of his "illustrious predecessors," Harcourt and Randolph Churchill, and Bevin was always keenly interested in details of the careers of past Foreign Secretaries. They evidently desired to be identified with those who had led Britain in an age when British preeminence was unquestioned.

With the partial exception of Dalton and Cripps, members of the Cabinet had first been attracted to socialism as a result of a conviction that more should be done to improve the lot of the poor. They may have flirted with the socialist concepts of internationalism and anti-imperialism, but their real motivation was to clear up the slums of London's East end or to improve the wages of cab drivers. They did not undertake intense or prolonged study of Britain's international position, and their earliest attitudes on this subject were not put under serious strain. Members of the Foreign Office with their more conservative outlook on life were even less prone than were their political counterparts to change their early attitudes towards their country.

It is true that from the time of the First World War there was an increasing awareness that Britain no longer possessed the strategic and economic power to impose her will on the world, as was evidenced by the appeasement of Germany in the late 1930s. However, even if at an action tendency level, there was some movement away from attitudes learned during schooldays, most other attitudes in the constellation of attitudes concerning Britain and her superiority remained unchanged.

NOTES

1. See above p. 8.

2. See, for example, Auld (1975) and Price (1972).

3. Thornton (1968) p. 270.

4. Plumb (1969) p. 86.

5. Quoted in Geyl (1970) p. 37. The most popular history book of the period was probably Green's *Short History of the English People*. Although its author was not so obviously patriotic as Macaulay, the theme of the book is nevertheless the manifest destiny of the English people.

6. Crisp (1945) p. 111.

7. Quoted in Steiner (1977).

8. Bryant (1934) p. 132.

9. For example, *British Industries and Foreign Competition* (London 1894) and particularly *Made in Germany* (London 1896).

10. Speech by President of National Liberal Foundation (1904), quoted in Thornton (1959) p. 105.

11. See Stokes (1962) p. 47.

12. Quoted in Bryant (1934) p. 133.

13. Le Feuvre (1911) pp. 8 11.

14. Quoted in Quayle (1973) p. 106. According to Quayle, this book was particularly popular among headmasters as a school prize.

15. Thornton (1968) p. 16.

16. Orwell, "Riding Down from Bangor", *Tribune*, 22 November 1946.

17. Baden-Powell (1909) p. 270.

18. Springhall (1977) p. 17.

19. Ibid., p. 19.

20. Quoted in Wilkinson (1964) pp. 101-2. See also Barnett (1972) p. 26.

21. See Steiner (1977) pp. 15-16.

22. Starr (1929) p. 21.

23. League of Nations International Committee for Intellectual Cooperation, The International Congress of Historical Science. For details, see Dance (1960) p. 127.

24. Scott (1926).

25. Starr (1929) pp. 33-34.

26. Attlee Papers, draft for "As it Happened" p. 14.

27. Ibid., p. 3.

28. Attlee (1961) p. 6.

29. Attlee Papers, draft for "As it Happened" p. 14.

30. Dalton (1953) p. 27.

31. See Senelick (1973).

32. Donoughue and Jones (1973) p. 11.

33. Shinwell (1955) p. 23.

34. Letter to author from Devon County Archivist (10 June 1977).

35. Strang (1956) p. 25.

36. Gladwyn (1972) p. 9.

37. Kelly (1953) p. 51.

38. Wheeler-Bennett (1976) p. 22.

39. Donoughue and Jones (1973) p. 31.

40. Ibid., p. 46.

41. Ibid., p. 112.

42. Ibid., p. 251.

43. Ibid., p. 253.

44. Ibid., p. 249.

45. Lapie (1971) p. 8.

46. Donoughue and Jones (1973) p. 482.

47. Ibid., p. 510.

6

Attitude Formation in Later Years

The previous chapter examined how basic attitudes with regard to Britain's role in world affairs were influenced by the policymakers' memories of events in their formative years. This chapter examines how these attitudes were influenced by their memories and interpretations of events in the years between their youth and the conclusion of the Second World War. It describes, in particular, how the policymakers perceived the economic and political tensions of the interwar years and the experience of the Second World War and discusses to what extent these perceptions affected the attitudes they adopted towards defining Britain's role in the postwar world.

PERCEPTIONS OF THE INTERWAR PERIOD

Whenever a war is over, postmortems begin. At every level of society, from the barber's shop to the learned academy, the question is asked: "How did it all come about?" In Britain, many found the answer in what they saw as the weakness and vacillation that had so characterized both domestic and foreign policy during the two decades after the close of the First World War. Criticisms of foreign policy were particularly acute; the "surrender of Munich," in particular, entered into the new history books as one of the most shameful episodes in British history.[1] *The Times*, which had supported appeasement and the Munich decisions, had set the tone when in a series of major articles in November 1943 it openly criticized the weakness and wishful thinking of British foreign policy in the 1930s and called for "a revival of national self-confidence" on which future British success could be built.

The future Cabinet Ministers used criticisms of the foreign policy of the interwar period as a studied part of their electoral tactics. A former member of the Labour Party research staff made this clear in a letter to Ernest Bevin in which he gave advice for the coming campaign:

> Smite them hips and thighs. . . Assail Conservatives tooth and nail. For past record of appeasement, continuance during the war of appeasers in important positions. . . For foreign relations conducted at high society level at home (Ribbentrop etc.) and abroad (embassies).[2]

From the outset of his career in Parliament, Bevin showed interest in establishing a stronger foreign policy. He told the annual conference of Labour candidates in 1940 that it would be no more possible to return "to the social and economic views of the 1930s after the war than to the policy of appeasement; both were equally discredited."[3]

In April 1945, in the speech at Leeds that made virtually impossible the longer continuation of the coalition government, he made a fierce attack on the "twenty wasted years" of Tory rule between the wars in which they had brought the country to the verge of disaster by their anxiety to cut a deal with Hitler.[4] Once in power at the Foreign Office, he often reminded his colleagues of the need to learn from the errors of the interwar governments; for example, in the Cabinet Defence Committee meeting of 7 November, 1945, he urged his colleagues not to repeat the error of cutting down on the armed services in peacetime.[5]

Attlee and Alexander, perhaps feeling rather vulnerable to counterattack, did not make many specific attacks on the conduct of interwar foreign policy. However, by the number of general criticisms of the period that they made, it is obvious that they saw the interwar years as a period of history that ought not to be repeated. Attlee's feelings were typically expressed in a speech given in Birmingham in 1946:

> After the last war this country failed to rise to the height of the occasion. There was inevitable war weariness, but to this was added a mood of cynicism, of selfishness and of hedonism. The ignoble slogan of "safety first" was preached and practiced.[6]

Alexander often admonished his listeners to learn from the lessons of the past, urging them in particular not to repeat "the timidity and vacillation" of the 1930s.[7]

One of the most forceful denunciations of the interwar period was made in the broadcast address of Philip Noel-Baker, who was later to join Bevin as a Junior Minister at the Foreign Office. After lambasting the Tories for allowing poverty and unemployment, he claimed:

It was the vacillation, the anarchic futility of Tory policy, which helped in great measure to bring the war. . . we promise that neither fear nor vacillation, nor the obstructive doubts of so-called "experts" nor the power of vested interests, nor the subterfuge of diplomacy, shall stop us.[8]

The Foreign Office officials did not need to win debating points about the past as did the politicians. However, although they did not make the same explicit and harsh criticisms of prewar foreign policy, there is evidence that they too resolved to make postwar policies firmer and stronger. The perceived failures of the past were largely influential in bringing about the reforms of the Foreign Office that Eden and Bevin put into force in the mid-1940s. Ashton-Gwatkin, one of the leading officials in charge of the implementation of the reforms, explained that the structural changes were designed to solve twelve problems that had made the Foreign Office incapable of coping with the difficulties of the 1930s.[9]

Finally, it might be asked whether, in the early postwar years, the trauma of depression and economic hardship in the 1930s might have predisposed the policymakers to reject costly big-power initiatives so as to conserve resources and help prevent a return to a similar depression. If so, did such a predisposition counterbalance the predisposition to increasing spending on foreign affairs that sprung from the perception of earlier foreign policy weakness? From the discussion of attitudes toward economic questions set out below in Chapter 8, it appears that this might have been the case with Dalton and officials at the Treasury but does not seem to have been so with other policymakers. The prevailing view seems to have been that the problems of the 1930s were not caused so much by overly high levels of government expenditures abroad as they were by the problems created by the inescapable consequences of international protectionism and the depressed world economy and by inappropriate domestic economic policy directions. The policymakers found grounds for hope that with the foundation of the United Nations Organization and particularly of the two Bretton Woods institutions--the International Monetary Fund and the International Bank for Reconstruction and Development--that a new era of international economic cooperation was beginning. As to domestic economic policies, the sharp fall in the rate of unemployment, the general rise in incomes during the war years, and the obviously high level of unsatisfied demand at the war's end provided evidence that, with suitable demand-management policies, it ought to be possible to achieve economic growth of a magnitude sufficient to permit the improvement of living standards as well as the maintenance of overseas responsibilities.

PERCEPTIONS OF THE SECOND WORLD WAR

     In the same way that memories of Britain's involvement in world affairs during the 1920s and 1930s gave rise to feelings of shame, memories of her involvement during the years of the Second World War gave rise to intense pride. It was true that the victory days that followed the defeats of Germany and Japan were not characterized by the great elation that had marked the celebrations of November 1918, but, significantly, there was no subsequent feeling of disillusionment that so quickly followed the end of the first world conflict. There was a deep feeling of satisfaction that Hitler had finally been defeated and that Britain had been a major cause--and in the view of most people *the* major cause--of his downfall. In fact, the general perception of Britain's war effort in the immediate postwar years tended to be rather romanticized. There was a feeling that the British armed services had been successful not because of the quantitative or qualitative superiority of their weaponry nor even because of the brilliance of their strategies but because, quite simply, they were British, and the British did not lose. Papers, speeches, and films of the day abounded in references to the country's "finest hour" and to the period when Britain had "stood alone" against seemingly insuperable odds.[10]

     This way of perceiving the war was not without its justification. Although it is arguable that the war had been as much lost by the Axis powers as won by the Allies, it is undeniable that the British people as a whole responded massively to the call to arms and by skillful organization played a major part in the ultimate victory. Whatever the true extent of Britain's contribution to the victory, the importance attributed to that contribution and to the perceived superiority of the British people was influential in the formation of attitudes regarding Britain's role and policies in the postwar world.

     The British people were already predisposed by their education and culture to view themselves as somehow superior to other peoples. Winston Churchill, the wartime leader, made conscious efforts to confirm those predispositions. Indeed, he is reported to have said to the American official, Henry Stimson, during the war, "Why be apologetic about Anglo-Saxon superiority; we are superior."[11] His masterful wartime speeches were widely listened to and were influential in forming or perhaps reinforcing a concept of British invincibility. His stirring rhetoric was reinforced by many other public figures and in a variety of ways. For example, George VI, whose messages to the nation were carried to almost every home by BBC radio, evoked powerful images of his courageous subjects who had "stood alone in the defence of freedom" and who "did not fail mankind in its hour of deadliest peril."[12] These two images of standing alone to defend freedom and of saving mankind were pervasive, appearing frequently in Cabinet Ministers' speeches.

Attlee as well frequently romanticized the British war effort, referring often to Britain having "stood alone in defence of freedom and civilization."[13] Bevin perceived Britain's contribution to the war in a similar manner. In 1945 he read the text of "Enemy Coast Ahead" by Guy Gibson, apparently in the generally Conservative *Sunday Express*, which had published it in serial form. The two major themes of the story were the bravery of British air crews and the success of the British in pulling off dramatic victories against overwhelming odds, in particular in the "dam-busting" mission. Bevin found the story "excellent," so much so that he requested an extra allotment of then strictly rationed paper so that in book form it could be guaranteed the widest possible dissemination.[14] Looking back on the war victory in his new position as Foreign Secretary, he told the House of Commons:

> Our own part is one of which we can be justly proud. History
> may well judge that our place is the proudest place of all. To
> the people of these islands belongs the imperishable fame of
> those grim days when, almost unarmed, they rose, refused to
> accept defeat, fought on, and made this little island the bastion
> of liberty. . . it can be fairly said that we held the fort and
> preserved the soul of mankind. Our policy now must be
> worthy of our people.[15]

In similar vein, Defence Minister Alexander spoke proudly of "the spirit which enabled us alone, with the company of our free sister nations of the Commonwealth about us, to defy the exultant hun."[16]

Among Foreign Office officials the view of the war was much the same. The guidelines given to Foreign Service officials in the United States summarized official thinking:

> The moral stature of Britain in the world has in no way
> diminished during the war. From the beginning we sustained
> the struggle against the Germans, against great odds; for we
> were little prepared for war. . . we fought in many lands and
> in the skies. From our gravely strained resources we nurtured
> those of our allies. . . we continued to play our full part--more
> than our full part--year after year. . . Our own people have
> come out of the war tired, but with their heads up.[17]

The attitude of Sir Alexander Cadogan was made clear in his diary entry of 15 August 1945 where he wrote, "The problems in front of us are manifold and awful. But I've lived through England's greatest hour, and if I can see no falling away from that, I shall die happy."[18] Other public servants influential in the foreign policy decision-making process had similar opinions. For example, Lord Keynes felt strongly that Britain deserved a generous American loan, because "for nearly two years the U.K. with her small population, having no support except the steadfastness of the distant members of the British Commonwealth, held the fort alone."[19]

Romanticized views of Britain's role in the war gave rise to a discernible increase in patriotism. Patriotism had been unfashionable in the intellectual climate of the interwar years, perhaps because patriotism in the form of belligerent nationalism was perceived to have been one of the major causes of the First World War. By 1945 the new acceptability of patriotism was but one example of the rehabilitation of Edwardian attitudes concerning Britain and its world role. Edward Shils, an American academic, who attempted to analyze the Labour Party's foreign policy some few months after they had taken office, seemed fascinated by the interplay between patriotism and the Labour view of Britain's role in the world:

> Accession to power at a moment when Britain's pride has been heightened and its material foundations weakened has led to a new sensitivity among Labourites about Britain's position in the world. Perhaps it was the experience of the war against Naziism which aroused in many young University men a kind of patriotism difficult to express--a patriotism which the spiritual residue of the disillusioning twenties and of the doctrinaire Marxist and Pacifist thirties made it painful to acknowledge.[20]

THE INTERWAR YEARS: A DISCONTINUITY IN THE FLOW OF BRITISH HISTORY

The rejection of the interwar period and the acceptance of a romanticized image of Britain's role in the war combined to give new value to attitudes learned during formative years. The policymakers' view of history was overwhelmingly Whig in its orientation; in simple terms, they saw the progress of Britain continuing up until the First World War, being halted in many areas or even being pushed back during the interwar period, and then continuing again from the moment of Churchill's assumption of the premiership and the evacuation of Dunkirk. These two events of May 1940 came to be seen as the moments when the vacillation and cowardice of the interwar period finally came to an end and when the British people began to assert themselves forcefully once again in the tradition of their pre-First World War ancestors. Dunkirk, the Battle of Britain and the victories of the Second World War aroused feelings about Britain that had not been felt since Edwardian days and breathed new life and vitality into the attitudes formed in the policymakers' schooldays. During this period it was not the world wars that provided the discontinuities in modern British history; it was more the period of peace that had come between them.

A clear expression of this perceived link between Britain post-1945 and an idealized Britain of earlier times was made by Alexander while Minister of Defence. After being invested with the LL.D of the University of Sheffield, he told the audience:

> We must have a great upsurge of the spirit with which Britain has always faced her most critical days. The spirit which defied the Inquisition in the days of Elizabeth was the spirit which welled up in us in our darkest hour in 1940. We need that spirit today.[21]

Attlee frequently turned his back on the events of the interwar years and alluded to the need to recapture the dynamism of the country's past. One of his favourite quotations, used as the peroration of many of his speeches during this period was taken from the works of John Milton:

> Methinks I see in my mind a noble and puissant nation rousing herself like a strong man after sleep, and shaking her invisible locks. Methinks I see her as an eagle mewing her mighty youth, and kindling her undazzled eyes at the full midday beam.[22]

Another favourite quotation often used by Attlee was taken from a work of Emerson, published in the 1840s, which said of Britain:

> She well remembers that she has seen dark days before; indeed with a kind of instinct that she sees a little better on a cloudy day, and that in storm of battle and calamity she has a secret vigour and a pulse like a cannon.[23]

This last quotation seemed a favourite with Cabinet Ministers. Dalton, for example, used it himself on several occasions.[24]

Bevin's personal memories of the years before 1914 were painful, and he did not romanticize that age in the same way as did Attlee and some of his other colleagues. It is nevertheless clear that Bevin felt that the role played by Britain in pre-First World War days was more appropriate for the Britain of the late 1940s than the one she had played during the interwar years. As he told the House of Commons in May 1947, "We still have our historic part to play. . . His Majesty's Government do not accept the view. . . that we have ceased to be a great power, or the contention that we have ceased to play that role."[25]

        In brief, there was a general tendency among those influential in making foreign policy decisions to regard the interwar period as an aberration or a discontinuity in the flow of British history. They hoped that they would be able to pick up the threads and move Britain along the correct path from which she had deviated soon after the end of the First World War. This meant that no longer could Britain be weak and given to appeasement; she had to be strong and thereby able to prevent the growth of any future threat to her security.

THE NEED FOR A STRONG FOREIGN POLICY

        The rejection of appeasement and the view that when the country asserted itself it could win victories against overwhelming odds led to the formation of a clearly discernible attitude that Britain should play an assertive leadership role in the postwar world. As Churchill argued, "Only a Britain that is strong and ready to fight in defence of freedom will count in the high councils of the world and thus safeguard coming generations against the immeasurable horrors of another war."[26]

        Views such as this were not merely political rhetoric, they were the reflection of a commonly held view. If in the past weakness and vacillation had led to the Second World War, then, logically, strength and preparedness to fight should ensure future peace. A study group of foreign policy and military experts, convened by the Royal Institute of International Affairs, reached the following conclusions in its report published in 1946:

> It is most important that the people of Britain should remember that this country can be a bulwark of peace only if she is strong. . . It should. . . now be a cardinal principle for Britain to maintain up-to-date defences in a much greater state of immediate readiness than has ever before been necessary. Time is no longer on her side: it has become the most unrelenting of neutrals.[27]

        The need for a stronger Britain with larger, better-prepared armed forces that would be used if necessary was felt by members of the Attlee Cabinet. When committing his views on foreign policy to paper in July 1944, Attlee was quite definite in his conclusion that Britain would need to shore up her strategic position so that she could play a proper role within the World Organization as the equal of America and Russia.[28] These attitudes were carried over into the postwar years during the period of his primeministership. The need for a strong and vigorous role for Britain was explained typically to a meeting of the Newspaper Society in May 1946. Having reviewed the areas in which British troops were active, Attlee continued:

> We must carry these commitments, including those in the
> occupied countries, because it is essential to the future peace
> of the world that we should not let go of the job to which we
> have set ourselves until the fruits of victory are made certain.
> To do so we must be strong and able to carry all those
> responsibilities which properly fall to us.[29]

Although Attlee certainly opposed any further significant expansion of
the British Empire and was even prepared to cut back on the British presence in
some areas, he was nevertheless deeply committed to the attitude that Britain
should continue to play a role of world leadership. Behind many of his speeches
it is not difficult to perceive the Attlee who marched triumphantly through the
streets when Ladysmith was relieved. Attlee now evidently wanted Britain to
play a strong role on the world stage and to break away from the cynicism,
lethargy, and weakness of the recent past.

Bevin also felt strongly that the lessons of the past pointed to the
necessity of Britain maintaining and increasing her strength in the postwar
period. Lord Longford who worked for him as a Junior Minister in the Foreign
Office recalled:

> I always thought he carried to exaggerated lengths the idea that
> the Germans respected strength above all things and that once
> we lost our reputation for strength through any apparent
> wavering of policy, we should lose with it the educational
> opportunity on which he was as keen as I was.[30]

In a contemporary comment on Bevin, Professor Epstein concluded that "What
was understood by way of the need for power in behalf of one's union
organization seems to have been readily transferred to the acceptance of strength
as an instrument of foreign policy."[31] This transference was evident in the case
of Greece. In August 1945 Bevin explained to the Cabinet Defence Committee
that he hoped to counter threats to Greek frontiers by diplomacy. He then added
in words that would not have been out of place in a briefing session for shop
stewards, "but it is essential that we should be able to support our diplomacy
with some show of strength." Bevin certainly agreed with the explicit objectives
of British foreign policy in Greece, namely preventing the coming to power of
a communist government. However, the major objective he had in mind was the
maintenance of an appearance of British strength and resolve so that Russia
would not be allowed to pursue the same type of expansionist policies that
British appeasement had allowed Germany to follow in the 1930s. He later
explained to the same meeting:

If the Russian challenge to our position in Greece and Turkey is successfully countered in its early stages, it is probable that the Soviet Government will not persevere in their present policy. But if they are successful in Greece, Turkey would be the next to go and an assault on our position in the Middle East would soon follow. The one thing which might encourage them to persevere in their present course would be for us to weaken in our determination to preserve Greece.[32]

Alexander very much shared Bevin's way of thinking. He vigorously opposed those who called for massive reductions in the strength of the armed forces. He told a Derby audience in 1947, "We shall never use our armed strength in an unjust cause, but we can not rely on preserving peace by weakness which merely tempts the aggressor." Britain needed to be strong, he explained, not only to ensure that the fruits of war victory were not squandered but also "so that Britain can speak in the councils of the nations with dignity and authority."[33]

The need for Britain to raise a stronger and more assertive voice was often expressed by Foreign Office officials, particularly in connection with the country's relations with Russia. Nigel Ronald, one of the Assistant Under-Secretaries of State, expressed his feeling that Britain should take a tough line in organizing some kind of Western bloc. Such a show of strength would go against Russian wishes but, paradoxically, could help Anglo-Russian relations by increasing the respect felt for Britain in the minds of the Russian leaders:

We must then disregard the Russians in framing our policy in this matter. And in so doing it may well be that we shall do no harm but good to essential Anglo-Russian relations. . . until the U.K. have [sic] a policy, they will continue to be pushed around by the Russians (and indeed by the Americans). Russia not only despises us for not knowing our own minds, she regards as quite useless to her allies, people who appear incapable of recognizing and standing up for their vital national interests.[34]

Some months earlier at the San Francisco Conference, Cadogan had asked himself what would be the best way to handle the Russians. After having recounted to his wife the details of one long and fruitless negotiating session, he wrote:

All this must be completely puzzling to you. It's simply arguing about words, on the surface, but it is of course a symptom of something much deeper--Russian suspicions and unwillingness to cooperate. How to cure those I really don't know. And I don't know whether it's better to have a good rough showdown with the Russians, or to attempt to go on coaxing them. I am inclined to think the former.[35]

Predictably perhaps, the leaders of the armed forces were convinced that the future world peace depended on Britain playing a much stronger and more positive role than she had played during the interwar period. Navy Chief of Staff Cunningham's diary is revealing in that respect; on 10 June 1945 he recorded:

De Gaulle has climbed down over Val d'Aosta and other places on the Franco-Italian frontier. Thus two messes [he was referring also to the Venezia Giulia dispute] have been cleared up by Anglo-American firmness, I hope the lesson will not be lost.

On 12 July 1945 he described the discussions that had taken place that day at the meeting of the Chiefs of Staff:

Much discussion on the paper on "security of the British Empire" by the post-war planners. A very pusillanimous document which talked mostly about retreat before the Russians.

His predilection for firm action affected his perception of specific foreign policy issues. For example, on 19 October 1945 he recorded, "I am myself convinced that with a show of force in Java all will be well."[36]

It should be remembered that Bevin remained in contact with Eden during the early postwar period and valued his advice. Eden, not unnaturally wanting to preserve his reputation of antiappeaser, advocated a strong line for British foreign policy. In a March 1945 Cabinet Committee meeting he had backed Bevin up in calling for continued conscription after the war. "Our foreign policy," he had said, "must be backed by sufficient military force if we wished to remain a leading power."[37] Cadogan recorded in his diaries that Eden had advised taking a hard line with Russia in the postwar conferences and that he was pleased that Bevin had been chosen as Foreign Secretary, no doubt because of his reputation for toughness in negotiations.

It was the general view of policymakers that if Britain wanted to live in peace and security in the future, then she had to act more firmly and positively in world affairs. They admitted that it might not be possible to reimpose a Pax Britannica, but felt that at least Britain should take the initiative and should encourage the United States and perhaps some other Western

European countries to stand resolutely against any further blatant threats to world order and peace.

Another component of the attitude that Britain should play a strong role in the postwar years was the perceived obligation to honour those who had died during the course of the war. If a society is to be successfully mobilized for war, then the population must see some purpose and need for such an action. People must accept at least a majority of their country's stated war aims. If they are victorious, the war aims are vindicated and become incorporated not only into the country's history books but, also, once the war aims have been effected, they form the basis of future foreign policy, the new status quo that needs to be preserved. Such was the case in Britain. The British people saw themselves going to war not only to liberate Central and Eastern Europeans from an oppressor but also to maintain Britain's imperial and world power status. The war had been long, and hardship had been suffered by most people; many lives had been lost, and even more had been blighted in some way. The knowledge that Britain, though victorious, had emerged from the war with a weaker world position was extremely difficult to accept, for if that were the case then all sacrifices would have been in vain. Churchill tried to play on the fear of this unthinkable possibility in his election campaign. He once told a radio audience:

> If our country dissolves into faction and party politics, we shall cease to fill the place won for us by our policy and our victories afloat and ashore, we shall cease to fill that place in the counsels of the nations which so much blood and sacrifice has gained. Without our aid the world itself might go once again astray.[38]

The need to give meaning to war sacrifices by maintaining a strong world power role for Britain was deeply felt by Attlee and his colleagues. While addressing both houses of Parliament in Ottawa he proclaimed, "It is for us to see that victory is not nullified by the failure to deal effectively with the problems of the peace. We owe it to the valiant dead that they shall not have died in vain."[39] Alexander, in late 1947, made a speech in which he called for Britain to act with "dignity and authority" in world affairs. He concluded:

> We must, for the time being, maintain sufficient defence forces if we are not to break faith with those who died for their country and their principles in the Second World War. Let us remember that perseverance keeps honour bright.[40]

The desire not to break faith with those who had died seems to have influenced his thinking on a number of matters. For example, while in Egypt in January 1946 he cabled Bevin, who was at a Paris conference, telling him not to diminish the British presence in the Middle East because it had been "paid for by British life and treasure."[41]

Bevin was motivated by the same desire to ensure that British sacrifices during the war had not been made in vain. As he told the House of Commons:

> I am not unmindful of the heavy responsibility that rests upon my shoulders. In conducting the foreign policy of this country I shall always be activated by the desire that it should be worthy of the immense sacrifices that have been made during the war.[42]

Earlier, during the war, Bevin had been moved to tears when, while watching the embarkation of troops for the D day landings, some of his union members had called out, "Look after the Missus and kids, Ernie."[43] Bevin, the old union negotiator, believed that what Britain had acquired through the sacrifices of its citizens should not be surrendered.

ATTITUDES UNDERMINING THE PURSUIT OF A STRONGER FOREIGN POLICY

The attitudes that Britain needed to be strong and to model her foreign policy decisions on those taken in a much earlier age when the country had been in the ascendant rather than on those taken in the shameful interwar period and that wartime sacrifices should not have been made in vain predisposed the policymakers to maintain as many overseas territories as possible and to strengthen the country's power in the running of the postwar world. However, the influence of these attitudes was modified to some extent by the existence of certain other attitudes, which, although they harmonized quite well at a cognitive and at an affective level with the attitudes previously described, exerted a neutralizing pressure at an action tendency level.

The first of these attitudes was that Britain deserved the rewards of victory. There was a deep feeling, one fueled by a constant stream of wartime propaganda, that the British people had by their privations, sacrifice, and valour won a resounding victory and that with the war over they deserved some rewards. It did not seem logical that the victory should be followed by a period of greater effort to bring about national prosperity; on the contrary, some relaxation had been earned, the need for greater effort had passed. This attitude affected directly the general psychological environment in which foreign policy decisions were created. The idea that the British people had earned the right to a more comfortable life by their war efforts was often voiced in the 1945 election campaign. Attlee in one of his election broadcasts claimed:

The men and women of this country who have endured great
hardships in the war, are asking what kind of life awaits them
in peace. They seek for the opportunity of leading reasonably
secure and happy lives and they deserve to have it.[44]

Cabinet Ministers often expressed indignation that Britain was not receiving the
deserts of her victory and all that had gone into it. Bevin accused the Americans
of not giving sufficient credit to British war efforts:

We have cut our civil economy and also our export trade to
the bone so that we could fight with all our resources. The
Americans may not like the comparison between the size and
consequences of our effort and theirs but the facts remain. . .
Americans would be indignant if we treated Egypt or India in
the way they propose to treat us.[45]

This sense of injustice and indignation was shared by Lord Keynes, who
was in charge of the team of British civil servants sent to negotiate with the
Americans. Analyzing Britain's postwar economic situation, he recalled how
Britain had "held the fort alone" and had made great sacrifices of energy,
manpower, and possessions. He then continued:

It cannot then appear to those who have borne the burden of
many days that it is a just and seemly conclusion of this
sacrifice to be left, as the price of what has happened, with a
burden of future tribute to the rest of the world, and mainly to
our own allies beyond tolerable bearing.[46]

This was admittedly a deliberate piece of forensic argument, but it was
nevertheless a reflection of Keynes's own attitudes. Whatever its merits, the
attitude that Britain deserved something on the strength of her past record rather
than on the strength of her future efforts encouraged a passive approach to world
affairs and probably made more difficult the necessary adjustment to the realities
of Britain's new diminished world status. As such it helped to counterbalance
the attitudes predisposing policymakers to adopt a more active and aggressive
stance in international affairs. Some historians feel that the effects of this
attitude can be seen in comparing Britain's halting postwar economic expansion
with the more robust economic expansion of Germany, where precisely the
opposite attitude was prevalent.[47]

Another attitude that effectively counterbalanced attitudes calling for a
strong and assertive stance in world affairs was the view that a country that had
so convincingly won a war under the most difficult circumstances could not
possibly fail to win the peace. For the new Cabinet Ministers it was

inconceivable that the British people with a peacetime government dedicated to its interests should fare less well than it had under the Tories during the war. Even before his nomination as Prime Minister, Attlee very obviously held a deep conviction that the country that had triumphed so gloriously in the war could not fail to win the peace. In his first election broadcast he told his audience that "the people who planned and carried through the Normandy landings will not be daunted by any difficulties."[48]   Attlee did not limit himself to such general declarations; rather, he applied this type of reasoning to a number of practical problems that faced the government. The attitude that the country that had won the war could not lose the peace seems to have clouded his mind to the serious long-term implications of Britain's postwar problems and the realities of Britain's decline as a world power. One can imagine the feeling with which he told the U.S. Congress, "We have not stood up to our enemies for six years to be beaten by economics."[49]

Bevin also evoked memories of Britain's success in the war and used them as evidence of the country's future success. He told the House of Commons at the end of 1945, during the debate on the American Loan:

> It was decision that carried us from 1940 to the end of the
> war. And it is decision that will carry us through now. . . We
> have to stand-to and try to carry great burdens. . . we stood
> together in 1940 and fought it through and Britain survived,
> and Britain shall still survive.[50]

The views of Attlee and Bevin were shared by Alexander, who in a speech in August 1947 gave a classic pronouncement of the line of reasoning: Britain is faced with seemingly insoluble problems; she did well in the war; therefore, she cannot fail to solve the problems in the peace.

> It may be that we are a bit the worse for wear, we may be
> shabby. . . we may have to face the novel position of a
> yawning gap between our earnings and what we want to buy
> in the world market, but you may be quite sure that the spirit
> which enabled us alone, with the company of our free sister
> nations of the Commonwealth about us, to defy the exultant
> Hun in 1940 will not be lacking now that we have to face the
> difficulties of a peacetime world.[51]

Certainly Cabinet Ministers reminded the British people often of their successes in the war and tried to persuade them to maintain what became known as the "Dunkirk Spirit" to win the problems of the peace. Crookshank, a former Conservative Minister, informed one audience in April 1946, "We are rapidly running into a financial and economic crisis, and Ministers are dashing about all over the country asking for unity and confidence in the world of productive industry. They want to revive the spirit of Dunkirk they say."[52]

Hugh Dalton was one of the greatest invokers of the Dunkirk spirit. In his crisis broadcast announcing the emergency economic measures of August 1947, he said:

> His Majesty's Government are confident in the future because we have confidence in you--the men and women of Britain--we are still the same people who showed the world what we could do, standing alone in days of war. Shall we do less to save ourselves in days of peace?[53]

For many it was inconceivable that the God who had brought Britain so successfully through the war would forsake them once the victory had been won. This powerful optimism prevented people from realizing or accepting the fact that British victory, even though divinely aided, had been paid for at a terrible cost to the British economy.

A final factor that enabled, or perhaps even compelled, Labour Ministers to maintain the attitude that Britain would succeed in peace as in war can be found in the attitudes of their political opponents. The great successes of the war, made more heroic month by month with the release of an increasing number of war films and radio programmes, had been achieved under Tory leadership. To have admitted that in the "easier" peacetime conditions Britain could not win comparable successes would have been a tacit admission of the superior ability of the Tories.

In conclusion, British policymakers were determined not to repeat the perceived mistakes of the past when weakness and vacillation had led to loss of position and war, and they were determined also to honour those who died and suffered during the war by ensuring that Britain's war aims were met, including notably the retention of the country's imperial and world power position. At an action tendency level, these attitudes were softened somewhat by the attitude that the war marked the end of the struggle and not the beginning of a new one; in other words, that it was not for Britain to struggle to establish a position of world importance because the rest of the world should recognize that she merited such a position by virtue of her valour and her performance from Dunkirk onwards. The motivation to take action to ensure the maintenance of British preeminence was also undermined by the attitude that a country that had won a major war against such overwhelming odds did not need to make radical changes to overcome any problems that peace could bring. All of these attitudes existed simultaneously, a fact that goes far to explain much of the hesitation in modifying traditional foreign policy stances in the early postwar years. The way in which the policymakers' attitudes distorted perceptions of Britain's real power in the postwar world was described by Shinwell, a member of the Attlee Cabinet, who, with the benefit of hindsight remarked:

> Like the majority of ordinary people, the Cabinet believed that the prestige earned by Britain's record in the war placed the country in the forefront of nations. This sense of pride clouded any realistic attitude to the fact that the war had produced two super-powers, and at the most Britain was only one of several great powers, and virtually bankrupt.[54]

NOTES

1. For example, E. H. Carr defended the Munich agreement in his book *The Twenty Years Crisis* published in 1939, calling it "the nearest approach in recent years to the settlement of a major international issue by a procedure of peaceful change". This and some other comments about the agreement were dropped entirely from the 1946 edition of the book.

2. Bevin Papers 2/14, letter from G. Mackenzie, 9 April 1945.

3. Quoted in Bullock (1967) p. 41. See also pp. 210, 275.

4. Ibid., p. 369.

5. PRO, Defence Committee Meeting, DO:45:13th meeting, 7 November 1945.

6. Attlee Papers, Box 21, Speech to the Annual Banquet of the Birmingham Jewelers and Silversmiths Association, 23 March 1946.

7. See, for example, Alexander Papers, Speech to the Institute of Pacific Relations, 1 September 1947.

8. Quoted in "The Listener," 21 June 1945, p. 689.

9. Ashton-Gwatkin (1949) pp. 23-24. For an interesting official admission of British weakness during the interwar period, see the record of the conversation between King Farouk of Egypt and Lord Altrincham, PRO PREM 8:82 (1945).

10. See Marwick (1968).

11. Thorne (1978) p. 730.

12. King George VI to his Peoples 1936-51 (1952). See particularly 25 December 1947.

13. See, for example, his speech in the House of Commons on 6 August 1947, Parliamentary Debates, volume 441, cols. 1487-1511.

14. Bevin Papers, File 6/59.

15. Parliamentary Debates volume 413, col. 300.

16. Alexander Papers, Speech to Royal Canadian Cadet Corps, 20 August 1947.

17. Attlee Papers, Correspondence with G. Mackenzie, January 1946; includes notes for British officials, Information Office, British Embassy, Washington D.C., 20 November 1945.

18. Dilks (1971) p. 782.

19. PRO, PREM 8/35, Communication from Keynes, 12 September 1945, Gen 89/1.

20. Shils (1945) pp. 511-512. See also Koestler (1943) pp. 227-243.

21. Alexander Papers, Speech at LL.D Investiture, University of Sheffield, 1 July 1947.

22. See, for example, his speech at the Lord Mayor's Banquet, 9 November 1946, Attlee Papers.

23. See, for example, his speech to both Houses of Parliament in Ottawa, 19 November 1945, Attlee Papers.

24. See, for example, his speech at the Mansion House, 9 October 1947, Dalton Papers.

25. Parliamentary Debates, vol. 437, col. 1965, 16 May 1947.

26. Quoted in the election address of Oliver Lyttleton, Chandos Papers.

27. Royal Institute for International Affairs (1946) pp. 17-18.

28. PRO, CAB 66/53 WP (44) 4/4 26 July 1944, "Foreign Policy and the Flying Bomb."

29. Attlee Papers, Speech to the Newspaper Society, 7 May 1946.

30. Pakenham (1953) p. 184.

31. Epstein (1954) p. 138.

32. PRO, D.O. (45) 4 (8 August 1945).

33. Alexander Papers, Derby War Memorial Speech, 27 September 1947.

34. F.O. 371: 59911, Z259/120/72, 1 January 1946.

35. Quoted in Dilks (1971) p. 747.

36. Cunningham Papers, Diary for 1945.

37. F.O. 371: 50805, U2105/173/70

38. Quoted in "The Listener," 5 July 1947, p. 17.

39. Attlee Papers, Box 19, Speech in Ottawa, 19 November 1945.

40. Alexander Papers, Derby War Memorial Speech, 27 September 1947.

41. Alexander Papers, File 5/11, Telegram to E. Bevin, 1 January 1946.

42. Parliamentary Debates (1945-46), vol. 413, col. 283.

43. Bullock (1967) p. 318.

44. Quoted in The Listener, 14 June 1945, p. 657.

45. PRO, PREM 8/35, Gen 89/8, Draft telegram to Washington, October 1945.

46. PRO, PREM 8/35, Gen 89/1, Lord Keynes, Proposals for Financial Arrangements in the Sterling Area and between the United States and the United Kingdom to follow after Lend-Lease, October 1945.

47. See, for example, Marwick (1963) p. 137.

48. Quoted in The Listener 14 June 1945 p. 660. See also Attlee Papers, draft letter to Patrick Gordon-Walker, September 1945.

49. Attlee Papers, Speech to U.S. Congress, 13 November 1945.

50. Parliamentary Debates, vol. 417, cols. 728, 736 (13 December 1945).

51. Alexander Papers, Speech to Royal Canadian Sea Cadet Corps, 20 August 1947.

52. Crookshank Papers, Speech at Annual Meeting of Lincoln National Unionist Association, 12 April 1946.

53. Dalton Papers, File IIc 9.1, Broadcast Speech, 20 August 1947.

54. Shinwell (1973) p. 183.

7

Public Opinion

Before concluding the analysis of the impact of contemporary factors on the formation of the policymakers' attitudes, some comments should be made on the role of public opinion. There is a large and growing body of literature on the influence of public opinion on foreign policy decision making.[1] Generally, in these studies, public opinion is a term used to refer to two interrelated but nevertheless separable phenomena. First, it refers to the attitudes held by the general population of a country; at this level, in very simple terms, public opinion can be said to support a particular policy if surveys indicate that more than half of the population is in favour of it. Second, the term *public opinion* refers to the views of particular pressure groups and the views of those who are powerful enough to have direct access to policymakers or whose authority commands respect.[2]

The debate on the influence of public opinion on foreign policy largely concerns the choice of a position on the continuum that has at one end the proposition that the beliefs of a largely uninterested and uninformed mass opinion are manipulated by policymakers who have definite views on the actions that need to be taken, and, at the other, the proposition that policymakers, and particularly those elected to office, have to follow the perceived wishes of the mass electorate.[3] In the predominantly U.S. literature on this subject, the escalation of the Vietnam war by the U.S. authorities is often cited as a reason for approaching the first end of the continuum, and the constraints imposed on policymaking in later years by the public's rejection of this war--"the Vietnam syndrome"--a reason for moving closer to the other end.[4] Both propositions clearly have value for analysis, and the relative importance of mass opinion versus elite opinion in the policy-making process is likely to fluctuate over time and particularly according to the degree to which the execution of foreign policy makes a noticeable impact on the standard or conditions of living of the general population.

Most studies of the early years of the first Attlee Government have tended to conclude that it was the policymakers themselves who charted the course of foreign policy and that they were little affected by public opinion. The statement of Kenneth Younger, who served as Minister of State in the Foreign Office under Bevin, has often been quoted to substantiate this point of view: "I was somewhat shocked to find out that I could not immediately recollect any occasion when I or my superiors had been greatly affected by public opinion in reaching important decisions."[5] However, this statement should not be taken to mean that the policymakers acted contrary to what they perceived public opinion to be; it could quite well mean that they were unaffected because foreign policy had relatively low salience for the general public, and public opinion was, in any event, generally supportive of the policy directions that they were taking.

Attlee accepted that a government could only legislate effectively when backed by "an informed and insistent public opinion." As he told one audience, "In peace as in war, governments can only act with success when the people which they represent want them to do so."[6] Attlee was not really a radical politician, and his policies were all set within the limits of what he perceived would be acceptable to the public at large. Although expressing his dependence on general public opinion, he claimed that he pointedly ignored any pressures from special interest groups. In a letter to Professor Robson, who had asked for information on the effects of pressure groups on his administration, Attlee replied:

> I fear that I have not any useful contribution to make on the subject. I never took any particular notice of them. I am not sure that I know what activities are comprised in those of pressure groups. I always refused to give pledges to any of the various groups that approached me at election time such as R.C.s, ex-servicemen, etc. so they ceased to bother me.[7]

It is interesting to note that the two pressure groups that first came to Attlee's mind--Roman Catholics and ex-servicemen--were groups exerting pressure to change domestic social policy rather than foreign policy.

Bevin, although often cavalier in his treatment of the opinions of party members, was conscious of the power of popular feeling, a consciousness he had not lost since the experiences of the General Strike. During the war he had opposed a general ban on horse racing on the grounds that "when a chap's thinking about who's going to win the 2:30 he isn't thinking about me."[8] As Foreign Secretary, Bevin was more relaxed with regard to public opinion. He felt confident that the public accepted his initiatives (a feeling justified by a number of opinion polls)[9] and took pride that he spoke for "the ordinary Englishman." Dalton was of the view that the British people were little interested in foreign affairs. The Tories, he wrote in his diary, were "making a good deal of hoot about India," but, he continued, "I don't believe that one person in a hundred thousand in the country cares tuppence about it, so long as British people are not being mauled about."[10]

Dalton exaggerated his point rather, but his Cabinet colleagues would have agreed with him that mass public opinion on foreign affairs only became vocal in the face of incidents that could be personalized in some way; for example, soft treatment of German war criminals or the hanging of two British sergeants in Palestine in 1947. Certainly, whenever mention is made of public opinion in Cabinet foreign policy discussions, it is in connection with the more emotive issues. For instance, in September 1945, the Cabinet decided not to push for too much industrial disarmament in Germany for fear of impoverishing the German people even further and setting up a possible humanitarian wave of British public opinion that would be difficult to handle.[11] The discussion on how many refugees the country would accept was largely influenced by public opinion considerations.[12] The effect of public opinion was also considered in relation to rather broader issues; for example, concern for the effects on public opinion of any seeming weakening of British authority with regard to India was a frequent subject of discussion. In June 1946, the Cabinet "took the view that having regard to current difficulties in Palestine and Egypt, it was important to avoid any course which could be represented as a policy of 'scuttle'. This would provide very strong reactions in this country and in the Dominions and would have a most damaging effect on our international position."[13]

The possible effects of public opinion were also taken into account by Foreign Office officials who were not unaware of the constraints popular feelings could impose on official policies. Many of them believed that the timidity of British foreign policy between the wars had, in part, been attributable to the weakness and defeatism of public opinion, which had made bolder policies impossible. In the immediate postwar years they were aware that public opinion was unlikely to sanction any radical departure from traditional foreign policy. In commenting on Professor Robbins's suggestion that Britain should take the lead in uniting Europe under British leadership, Orme Sargent wrote tersely, "Mr. Robbins is an Imperialist. The British proletariat is not. It is interested in the Beveridge Report, not in international planning. We must fashion our foreign policy accordingly.[14]

Earlier chapters have illustrated the similar nature of the attitudes concerning foreign policy held by the policymakers and those expressed by influential members of society. There was a similar compatibility between the attitudes of the policymakers and those of ordinary people. The polls taken by the British Institute of Public Opinion during the period demonstrate that foreign policy had very low salience among the public at large. In July 1945, with the war in the Pacific not yet over, only 8 percent of the public saw foreign affairs as the most important issue in the coming general election--a fact that may go far to explain why the Labour Party with its greater emphasis on domestic policy won such a resounding victory.[15] Even less importance was attributed to foreign policy as the months wore on. When in 1947, with the cold war underway, people were asked to name the most urgent problem facing the government, only 3 percent mentioned the overall postwar crisis, and even among those some were probably thinking more of domestic than of foreign issues.

Although foreign policy had very low salience in people's concerns, when they were questioned on specific issues they demonstrated that they still perceived Britain in her traditional leading imperial role. A public opinion survey commissioned by the Colonial Office soon after the war found that even during that period of austerity, only 16 percent of those questioned expressed unqualified disapproval to the question "Is it right to spend British taxpayers' money on Colonial development and welfare?"[16] Replies to other questions demonstrated a great ignorance of imperial questions but, nevertheless, great support for Britain's leading world role. The findings of such surveys can be confirmed by a study of those journals and letters of ordinary people in this period that are available for study.[17] An analysis of the collection of documents of this type held by the Imperial War Museum in London reveals much greater preoccupations with problems of jobs, rationing, and other domestic concerns than with problems of foreign affairs. The public were tired after six long years of war and austerity and felt that Britain's victories in the war had earned her a place of preeminence in the world. Pride at being a citizen of a great world power served to alleviate in some way the depressing conditions of the postwar years. The pride resulted not from profound reflection but from a nationalistic education reinforced by the rhetoric and propaganda of the war. In many cases this pride was not conscious; Professor Frankel concluded that "most Britons unconsciously continued to think about the immediate post-war world in terms of a Pax Britannica."[18]

The lack of constraints imposed by public opinion on the policymakers was attributable not so much to the low salience of foreign policy in people's thinking, therefore, as it was to the fact that overall assumptions and objectives were shared. There was a particularly wide consensus that Britain should maintain her role of world leadership. Had Bevin taken steps to withdraw Britain from all of its overseas commitments and to push the country into some supranational European union or had he tried in some other way to alter Britain's traditional world role, then public opinion might have been far less accommodating.

NOTES

1. There is a particularly useful summary of this debate in Chapter 8 of Wittkopf (1990). For an informative bibliographical essay on the subject, see Holmes (1985).

2. For a description of the different "publics" see "The Many Publics and the Few," Chapter 1 of Levering (1978).

3. A good example of the argument that elites set the framework to which the general public responds is set out in Ginsberg (1986).

4. See, for example, Wittkopf (1990).

5. Quoted in Frankel (1975) p. 40.

6. Attlee Papers, Box 18, Speech to United Nations Assembly, 10 October 1945.

7. Attlee Papers, Box 1, Letter to Professor W. A. Robson, 24 October 1957.

8. Quoted in Bullock (1967) p. 123.

9. See *Public Opinion Quarterly* 10 (1946) p. 135.

10. Dalton Diary, 6 February 1947.

11. See PRO, CM 31 (45) 13 September 1946.

12. See PRO, CM 49 (45) 6 November 1945 and CM 69 (46) 18 July 1946.

13. PRO, CM 55 (46) 5 June 1946.

14. Quoted in Gladwyn (1972) p. 120. The Beveridge report proposed the enactment of a number of social reforms notably with regard to health and social security.

15. *Public Opinion Quarterly* 9, no. 3 (1945).

16. 62 percent replied yes; 16 percent no; 10 percent don't know; and 12 percent gave a qualified answer. Quoted in Evens (1948) pp. 1-16.

17. See the archives of the Imperial War Museum; notably the diaries of Margaret Crompton and of Dr. J. P. MacHutchison and the Strong collection of letters.

18. Frankel (1975) p. 222.

Part 3

The Economic Setting

8

Attitudes and the Perception
of Britain's Economic Situation

Before examining how the attitudes of the policymakers affected individual foreign policy decisions, it is essential to examine how they affected perceptions of Britain's economic situation. A sound foreign policy requires a sound understanding of a country's economic capacity. If the policymakers' perception of Britain's economic situation in the years after the war was flawed, it could mean that there was a high risk that the foreign policy decisions they took could have been fundamentally inappropriate.

The parlous state of the the British economy with its major loss of export markets, deepening current account deficit, growing debt burden, and generally seriously weakened economic infrastructure was described in Chapter 1. This chapter also made reference to the view of many economic historians that, given the high, unsatisfied level of consumer demand at the end of the war and the great need for construction and investment throughout Britain, an earlier demobilization of servicemen and the earmarking of more dollars for imports of raw materials and intermediate goods would have strengthened Britain's economic base significantly and could well have helped Britain avoid the relative economic decline of the ensuing decades. Dalton and his officials at the Treasury tried incessantly to bring other Cabinet members and other ministries to understand the new economic realities and to appreciate that cutbacks in overseas expenditures were not only advisable but essential.

Even before the end of the war Keynes had repeatedly condemned anybody who advocated what he called "a rich uncle" role for Britain in the peace. In August 1945, he prepared for the new Cabinet a paper dealing with Britain's overseas financial prospects. After presenting a few facts and figures he went on to warn that to "undertake liabilities all over the world and slop money out to the importunate represents an overplaying of our hand."[1] The

Treasury in an associated briefing had recognized that Britain's receiving vast
supplies free of cost from the United States "enabled us to play a strategic and
diplomatic role throughout the world which would otherwise have been beyond
our power."[2]

Some six months later Keynes appeared exasperated that his advice had
not been better heeded. In a Cabinet paper he wrote, "The current and
prospective demands upon us for political and military expenditure overseas have
already gone far beyond the figure which can, on any hypothesis, be sustained."[3]
Public opinion would be angered, he said, if it became generally known that the
American loan and other resources were being used "to feed and sustain allies,
liberated territories and ex-enemies, to maintain our military prestige overseas
and, generally speaking, to cut a dash in the world considerably above our
means."[4]

Keynes's warnings were echoed by Dalton, who wrote to the Cabinet
in 1946:

> I must solemnly warn my colleagues that, unless we can reduce
> our overseas military expenditure drastically and rapidly and
> avoid further overseas commitments, we have no alternative
> but to cut our rations and reduce employment through
> restrictions in the import of machinery and raw materials.
> There is no way round this arithmetic and all our overseas
> policy must be conditioned by it.[5]

Although he often differed forcefully with Cripps, Dalton united with
him to try to bring home to fellow Cabinet members the seriousness of Britain's
economic situation. Dalton recorded in his diary for 29 November 1946 a
description of his resistance to demands for greater outlays in Greece, Turkey,
and Afghanistan: "We have not got the money for this sort of thing." He then
went on to record,

> Alarm and despondency over the prospects likely to arise at the
> end of two years, unless our supply of dollars can somehow be
> built up is well based. Cripps is making the public running on
> this, and I am trying to frighten my colleagues about it. This
> is much the most serious of my departmental headaches.[6]

A few weeks later, he noted, "I constantly tell my colleagues we shall be on the
rocks in 2 years time, if we have exhausted the Canadian and US loans unless
we have severely cut down our overseas expenditure."[7] The following month
in a letter to Attlee, he wrote:

> This huge expenditure of manpower and money on Defence is
> making nonsense of our economics and public finance. I was
> astonished at the blank wall I met both from you and Albert
> [Alexander]. . . I had hoped for a reasonable compromise. I
> thought I offered one.   I don't care for unconditional
> surrenders as a habit.[8]

He then went on to threaten resignation, saying, "I had much sooner be
out of it all and free to speak my mind if all my arguments are to be swept aside
like flies."   In a later diary entry, as he reflected on Britain's tangled
commitments in the Middle East and the constant demands for money that they
entailed, he wrote, "we are totally overstretched at present and just can't keep it
up."[9] A few weeks later, he sent yet another "short and scorching paper" to the
Cabinet to try to "frighten" them into some action.[10]

Dalton and the Treasury were not alone in putting forward this point of
view; many other influential voices called for adjustments that would make
Britain's overseas objectives commensurate with her resources.[11] No member
of Attlee's Cabinet and no leading official in the Foreign Office could claim to
be in ignorance of Britain's grave economic situation nor of the view of the
Treasury, not to mention other parties, that overseas expenditure would have to
be cut if the home economy was to be properly restored and given a healthy
foundation for success vis-à-vis its trading competitors. On occasion Dalton
would express contentment that his point of view seemed to have been heard and
accepted by the policymakers. Writing of Attlee in early 1946, he was obviously
happy that he was "getting him more and more aware of the overseas deficit.
Clearly the Keynes paper has done good."[12]

One of Bevin's most often quoted statements was his acknowledgement
that "If I had three million tons of coal which I could export. . . I could do
something effective.   I could have a foreign policy."[13]   Alexander also
recognized the constraints that followed the country's impoverishment.

> As in other matters at the present time, we just cannot afford
> the forces we would normally deem necessary, so while aiming
> to secure the best we can with the money available we have to
> be content with something below what, in better times, we
> should feel compelled to maintain.[14]

Returning to the definition of attitudes set out in Chapter 2, it can be
said that even though economic constraints on foreign policy were accepted at
a cognitive level, they were not necessarily accepted at an affective or an action-
tendency level. Dalton became increasingly frustrated that Attlee and senior
Cabinet Ministers refused to take action to cut back on overseas commitments,
the need for which they accepted at a cognitive level. In his view, this lack of

congruence between the different components of their attitudes represented "easy-going, muddle-headed irresponsibility."[15]   A prime example of this irresponsibility, the Chancellor felt, was the "mulish resistance" that Bevin, Alexander and, to some extent, Attlee offered to his suggestion that troop levels should be more rapidly reduced in order to alleviate labour shortages and give a boost to national productivity and income.

At a cognitive level the officials at the Foreign Office also acknowledged Britain's diminished economic strength. This is exemplified in the deliberations over the draft reply to be made in the House of Lords to a question from Lord Derwent in February 1945. Derwent was concerned at what he saw as a general feeling that because of the "material prodigalities of America and Russia," Britain would no longer be able to play a predominant part in world affairs. His question, in effect, asked whether the government shared that view. A reply was drafted by Ward, Falla, Coulson, and Professor Webster:

> In speaking of this country's contribution to economic reconstruction, however, it is necessary to utter a word of warning. The extent of our contribution will obviously be governed by that of our economic and financial resources, and it must not be forgotten that the resources which we possessed before the war have been very greatly depleted in the interests of victory and of the United Nations. It is clear that in considering this country's contribution to post-war economic revival, full account will have to be taken of our altered financial position and of the fact that our first need will be for reconstruction at home.[16]

Cadogan's diary entry at the Potsdam Conference in August 1945 makes quite clear that the then leader of the Foreign Office recognized some of the realities of the postwar world: "Big 3 (or 2 1/2!) at 4. Sat till about 7."[17]

Dixon, who as the Secretary of State's private secretary was close to Bevin, reflected on the country's new limitations in his diary in October 1946:

> The days are past when we could treat Egypt de "haut en bas" and act as a great power using a little power's territory for our own purposes as and when we judged our interests required it. . . If we wanted to maintain our old position of treating Egypt as a dependency or quasi-colony, we could only do so by the exercise of force and we no longer have the force or the wish to act that way.[18]

Various Foreign Office files also make clear the officials' recognition that the country's resources were not sufficient to finance some desired overseas objectives. For example, some officials observed that more economic assistance to the East European countries could help to swing the scales against Russian influence but were forced to recognize that the resources for such interventions were simply not available.[19] However, while the officials acknowledged that economic constraints made it impossible for the country to undertake significant new commitments, they did not go so far as to give serious consideration to cutting back on existing commitments. The fact of economic weakness was accepted at a cognitive level, but that acceptance was not translated into action, or at least not into action that was substantial enough to satisfy the Treasury.

It could, of course, be argued that the policymakers cut back as much as possible while still maintaining the defence of Britain and British interests; that, after all, India was given its independence and that there was a significant scaling down of British involvement in Greece, Egypt, Palestine, and other areas. It could be argued in return, however, that British withdrawals overseas were motivated not by strategic choices but overwhelmingly by external pressures or, as in the case of Greece, by the need for significant increases in expenditure that the Treasury was simply unable to meet. In considering foreign policy both Cabinet and Foreign Office leaders thought primarily of maintaining Britain's world power and not of reducing overseas expenditure in the interests of shoring up the country's weakened domestic economic base.

THE RESISTANCE TO REDUCING OVERSEAS EXPENDITURE

The constellation of attitudes that predisposed the policymakers towards the maintenance of the status quo was reinforced by certain conditions in the external environment in the postwar years. Firstly, although Russia had a frightening potential power, she was in practice still rather weak in 1945; there was no Russian atomic bomb, and the country was in the throes of massive political and economic reorganization. Secondly, all the states of the European continent were in an even weaker state than was Britain. Germany and Italy had been defeated and France, and the other states of Western Europe would long be engaged in overcoming the effects of enemy occupation. As for other potential world rivals, Japan had just been shattered by the first use of atomic bombs, and China was wracked by civil unrest. Thirdly, there were grounds for belief that leadership of the empire and commonwealth would guarantee for Britain a preeminent position in the international system.

To Attlee, Bevin, and the Foreign Office, these facts justified the hope that Britain could continue with the minimum of change to its world role. For Dalton and the Treasury none of these facts could mask the reality that Britain was able to continue playing her world role only by using the financial and other resources that were being received on loan from the United States; in their view, the domestic sector of the economy could develop satisfactorily only if some resources were transferred away from government foreign expenditure.

The desire to maintain Britain's world position was also reinforced by a number of pressure groups, but notably by the Tory Party and the military leaders. Churchill and other Tory officials often equated any diminution of Britain's overseas presence with treachery. This type of argument was particularly effective with Bevin and Attlee, concerned as they were to establish the image of the Labour Party as a credible, rational, and patriotic party, and not as a party that owed ultimate allegiance to Russia. Churchill frequently argued that true patriotism could only be reflected in decisions designed to strengthen the empire and build Britain's prestige abroad. At the 1946 Conservative Party Conference he attacked what he saw as Labour's overemphasis on achieving success in the domestic sector: "The British race is not activated mainly by the hope of material gain. Otherwise we should long ago have sunk in the ocean of the past." Labour's policy priorities could only be evidence of their fundamental lack of patriotism, he continued"

> Peering ahead through the mists and mysteries of the future as far as I can see it would seem that the division of the next election will be between those who wholeheartedly sing "The Red Flag" and those who rejoice to sing "Land of Hope and Glory." There is the noble hymn which will rally the wise, the sober-minded, and the good to the salvation of our native land.[20]

During a period when patriotism had taken on renewed importance, those taking foreign policy decisions would, at least, have had to have been aware of this type of criticism. Bevin and Attlee were more anxious to accommodate the criticisms of the Tory Party and those generally on the political right than they were those emanating from the left wing of their own party or other voices from the same part of the political spectrum. Certainly they were more often and more publicly hostile to the criticisms of the left. The fact that the left supported a scaling down of British overseas commitments probably made Bevin, in particular, more anxious to maintain them. It has been shown experimentally that an individual has a tendency to react against attitudes held by adversaries and to form attitudes of his own that are, if not diametrically opposed, at least radically different.[21] Bevin's feelings of enmity towards the Party's left wing and the socialist intellectuals are well known; his cavalier treatment of his parliamentary foreign policy advisory group has already been noted.[22] Attlee's position is well illustrated by an exchange of correspondence he had with Konni Zilliacus, an M.P. later to be temporarily expelled from the Labour Party for the unacceptably left-wing nature of his views.

Zilliacus wrote saying that he was "very much troubled indeed at our foreign policy and at the shape of things to come if we don't change it in time." Attached to the letter was an eight-page paper entitled "The Labour Government's Foreign Policy." The paper began very reasonably by pointing out that in June 1946 Britain would still have over 2 million men in the armed forces, which would be more than the Americans, and that peacetime expenditure on the armed forces would be in the order of £2 billion, with demands on manpower that would necessitate universal conscription of several years' duration. He then went on to comment:

> On January 29th Mr. Attlee declared that we could not speed up demobilization or cut down our establishments still further because of our world peace commitments. The plain truth is that we must either share these commitments with others. . . or else cut them by acts of unilateral abandonment. We can in no circumstances shoulder the burden indefinitely of foreign commitments, whether Imperialist or international, to the tune of £2,000,000,000 a year. If we attempt to do it we shall wreck our reconstruction programme and court the danger of economic and financial collapse.

The fears expressed by Zilliacus were worthy of a detailed response. If there was any substance to them, some action would seem to be called for. However, in his handwritten reply, Attlee said dismissively:

> My dear Zilly,
> Thank you for sending me your memorandum which seems to me based on an astonishing lack of understanding of the facts.
>   Yours ever,
>   Clem[23]

The reply probably related above all to Zilliacus's recommendations to accept the new great power role of the Soviet Union and the increased influence of the communist parties elsewhere in Europe and to phase out the British presence in Greece and in the Middle East. Noticeably, however, the question Zilliacus raised as to whether Britain could afford the projected defence expenditure was not addressed.

Pressure to maintain overseas expenditure was also exerted on the political leaders by the military leaders, who were anxious to play their part in postwar policy making. In their view, it was inaction by the politicians and civil servants that had made the last war inevitable, and it was important that, in the peace, decisions were taken that would ensure that the country was never again reduced to the relative military weakness of the 1930s. As Lord Tedder, who replaced Lord Portal as Chief of Air Staff, warned an audience in May 1946, "Don't let us make the mistake we made the previous time and let things slide."[24]

The story of the military leaders' resistance to cuts in defence and overseas expenditure emerges clearly from Admiral Lord Cunningham's diary. When the nature of Britain's desperate economic situation became evident in mid-August 1945, Cunningham felt that the possible implications for defence spending seemed "ominous."[25] At the beginning of September, when Attlee suggested cutting back any British role in the Italian colonies, his reaction was strong and immediate:

> The PM misreads the lessons of the war--practically preaches unilateral disarmament and advocates not putting our claim for trusteeship of Cyrenaica and Greater Somalia. I briefed the 1st Lord heavily and Warldeck produced another most trenchant brief.[26]

Two weeks later, he again criticized the Prime Minister:

> Discussed COS estimate of forces required to meet our commitments in June 1946. Attlee at his Little Englander worst. Why did we want garrisons in Gibraltar, Malta, Cyprus, Mauritius, etc.? What good were the West Indies and Bermuda to us, etc.
>
> If he has his way we shall have another unilateral disarmament stunt. George Hall [Colonial Secretary] spoke to me afterwards much upset by Attlee's attitude.[27]

The Chiefs of Staff were also at odds with the Foreign Office on these issues. Concerning a Chiefs of Staff meeting in March 1946, Cunningham recorded: "We turned down several of the FO suggestions particularly as regards reducing the size of the Greek army."[28] Another diary entry makes obvious that, however blunt and direct were the Chancellor's pleadings for a transfer of resources from foreign to domestic expenditures, they had little effect on Cunningham: "The Chancellor made a violent speech crying havoc. It was the usual excellent demonstration of trying to eat your cake and have it."[29] In Cunningham's view, rather than asking about the needs of the domestic economy, "surely the question should be can we afford not to have reasonable armed forces?"[30]

The foreign policymakers were in a dilemma: on the one hand, there were several voices proclaiming that Britain's long-term interest and power position depended on a transfer of scarce resources from foreign to domestic expenditure; and on the other, equally respectable voices were calling for the maintenance of as many as possible of the trappings of world power. On the whole--at a cognitive level--Attlee, Bevin, and the other policymakers had some attitudes favouring the reduction of overseas expenditure, but any tendency to act upon these attitudes was generally more than counterbalanced by other earlier learned attitudes exerting an influence at both a cognitive and an affective level and reinforced by the external factors mentioned earlier in this chapter. The dilemma in which they found themselves was perceptively analyzed by an American academic in summer 1945:

> In sheer power, it is clear, Britain no longer stands in the very front rank, and British foreign policy must reconcile and adapt itself to that fact. . . not the least of the post-war trials through which the British must pass is that of adjusting themselves psychologically to this unfamiliar condition.[31]

How did the policymakers adjust themselves psychologically to Britain's new unfamiliar condition? How did they balance contradictory attitudes? In Chapter 2, it was explained that individuals are able to live with relatively high degrees of cognitive dissonance, that is, they are able to accommodate themselves psychologically in order to maintain two or more cognitions that are obviously incompatible. As cognitive dissonance increases in degree, the individual is forced into behaviour directed towards its reduction. Complete relief from the pressures created by the dissonance can be obtained by repudiating one cognition, but perhaps more often--and this was certainly the case with the Attlee Government--the pressures are dissipated by modifying and frequently distorting one or both cognitions in order to blur the points of dissonance. The knowledge that resources needed to be diverted away from foreign to domestic expenditures did lead to action in some areas, such as the decision not to escalate British participation in the troubles in Greece and Turkey in 1947, but all too often the motivational pressure created by that knowledge was counterweighed by well-entrenched attitudes that Britain should continue to play a leading world power role, and it was dissipated before actions could be affected.

Attlee and the leaders of his Cabinet often dissipated their anxieties about Britain's economic position by falling back on a general feeling of optimism for the future, a feeling that things had often looked bleak for Britain before, as they had in 1940, but that solutions to problems had always turned up, and things had worked out in the end. However much the evidence of the structural changes in the world economy that had taken place to Britain's disadvantage reinforced Attlee's acceptance of British weakness at a cognitive level, he could not rid himself of the brighter visions of British preeminence that were deeply entrenched at an affective level: "We are having and will have many difficulties to overcome, but I am certain we shall win through. . . this country has a great mission today."[32]

Bevin's attitudes were similar. He saw Britain's weakness as an essentially temporary phenomenon; Barclay, who had worked with him very closely, recalled: "Ernie recognized that Britain had emerged with greatly diminished power as a result of nearly five years of war, but I am not sure that he fully grasped to what an extent we had been permanently weakened."[33] Alexander shared the outlook of his colleagues:

> The heart of Britain beats soundly yet, as soundly as ever it did. Difficulties such as we face just now exist for us only to be surmounted. We shall surmount them and we are putting our backs into the task that lies before us.[34]

That these speeches were not merely an expression of platitudes designed to give hope to a people that had seen little relief from wartime privations but an expression of the speakers' real attitudes is evident in some of the entries from Dalton's diaries. Dalton was the one Minister who clearly believed that Britain's economic problems were not merely transient but reflected a structural change in international relationships. He recorded how his efforts to convince the Cabinet leaders that Britain would not recapture her former economic capacity and would, therefore, need to reduce her world role met with "mulish resistance."[35]

One contemporary writer, who had predicted that Britain would find it difficult to adjust to a position behind the front rank of world powers was intrigued by the deep-seated yet barely justified optimism of the early postwar days. British morale, he concluded, was

> the result of complicated historical forces, and under some conditions it can take forms which the foreigner finds baffling and even annoying in its innocent assumption of superiority. . . in essence British morale is simply the conviction, rational or irrational, that Britain has always come out on top and any other issue would be unthinkable. The less promising the outlook, the higher British morale will probably rise.[36]

Another way that the officials dissipated the motivating effects of the cognition that Britain needed to transfer resources from the foreign to domestic expenditures was to focus on the country's moral power. In their view, although economically weakened and unable to rule the seas as in centuries past, Britain still had to fulfill its responsibilities of world moral and political leadership. In the words of one Conservative Party publication of the time: "The British Commonwealth has greater resources of political experience than any other nation. . . British leadership is more vital to the future of civilization now than at any time in history."[37]

Similar sentiments were expressed by Labour Party voices; Woodrow Wyatt, who in the 1945 Parliament was a vocal left-winger, wrote:

> Britain has passed the days in which she was great through domination by force. But there is opening to her, if she will grasp the chance, an era of greatness unparalleled in her history--a greatness which can come through the exercise of her harmonizing skill, of her capacity to make nations understand and tolerate each other's foibles. . . she has proved that material power is not all.[38]

Attlee frequently acknowledged Britain's moral superiority. He was convinced that Britain's major role after the war was to set the world an example of democracy in action:

> It is for us to show that the British way of life, with its freedom and democracy, with its kindliness, and with its acceptance of the moral values on which alone true civilization can be founded, can in peace as in war be an example to the whole world.[39]

Switching from economic and military leadership to moral leadership did not, however, involve switching resources from foreign to domestic expenditures, as Attlee made clear:

> It is essential that the voice of Britain and of the democratic way of life for which Britain stands should be heard with authority in international councils, and it will not be heard with that authority if it is believed that Britain is either unable or unwilling to carry out her international commitments even though at heavy cost to her resources.[40]

Bevin also spoke often of Britain's moral preeminence; in fact, such views, he felt, should transcend party differences:

> There is one thing about this country and this House, and that is that however much we disagree on whether we have enough houses or fried fish shops, we seem to agree on the imperative necessity of Britain retaining her moral lead in the world.[41]

The moral preeminence of the British people was a recurring theme in the speeches of King George VI. He told a Guildhall audience in 1947 that Britain's

heroic and tragic sacrifices and the new moral prestige which
has come to her, have prepared her for a new role in world
affairs. In the supreme councils of the world, she speaks not
merely with an authority based on physical force and war
potential, but also with a moral authority, and with an
unrivaled experience in the handling of men and human
affairs.[42]

J. H. Huizinga, a Belgian journalist who lived in England throughout
this period, summed up what he saw to be the attitude of most Britons:

How ready they showed themselves to claim the world's moral
leadership in and out of season, or to rub in the debt of
admiration owed to them for their steadfastness in their finest
hour by endlessly intoning the old theme song "we stood
alone."[43]

In conclusion, evidence that the British economy would benefit from a
transfer of resources from foreign to domestic expenditures was clearly apparent.
The motivation to take the action required by this knowledge was dissipated in
a number of ways, but notably by a vague optimism that Britain would in some
way be able to maintain her international position whatever the statistics
indicated. Moreover, any anxiety caused by evidence of Britain's declining
military or economic power was dulled by the feeling that the country should
continue to exercise its unparalleled moral leadership. In this light, it is easy to
understand why Dalton should have been moved to accuse his colleagues of
"muddle-headed irresponsibility." Finally, this chapter should not be read as
arguing that Britain should, overnight, have withdrawn all her troops and put an
end to all the expenses involved in administering a still substantial empire; it is
difficult even today to say exactly where and when the line should have been
drawn, which commitments should have been maintained, which scaled down,
and which abandoned. What this chapter has, however, pointed out is that the
policymakers were unwilling to address these questions fully and objectively.

NOTES

1. PRO, CP 45: 112.

2. PRO, Gen 89: 1, 1945.

3. PRO, CP (46) 58, 8 February 1946.

4. Ibid.

5. Ibid.

6. Dalton Diary, 29 November 1946.

7. Ibid, 20 December 1946.

8. Dalton Papers, Letter to C. R. Attlee, 20 January 1947.

9. Dalton Diary, 6 February 1947.

10. Ibid, 21 March 1947.

11. See, for example, Royal Institute of International Affairs (1946) p. 157; Hankey Papers, HNKY 14/15, Exchange of Correspondence between B. H. Liddell Hart and Lord Hankey; Shaw (1974) p.126; New Statesman, 7 September and 7 December 1946, 11 January, 20 July and 1 November 1947; and Orwell (1968) p. 398.

12. Dalton Diary, 9 February 1946.

13. Quoted in MacDonald (1976) p. 112.

14. Alexander Papers, Speech to Bradford and District Royal Naval Association, 25 October 1947.

15. Dalton Diary, 17 January 1947.

16. PRO, FO/371/50817, U/1183/396, 13 February 1945.

17. Dilks (1971) p. 778.

18. Dixon Diary, 7 October 1946.

19. See PRO, FO/371/53019, UE4006/413/53, 30 August 1946.

20. Quoted in Conservative Political Centre (1950), Speech at Blackpool, 5 October 1946.

21. Halloran (1967) p. 91.

22. See Chapter 2.

23. Attlee Papers, Letter from K. Zilliacus and Reply, February 1946.

24. Reported in *The Times*, 28 May 1946.

25. Cunningham Diary, 17 August 1945.

26. Cunningham Diary, 3 September 1945.

27. Cunningham Diary, 14 September 1945.

28. Cunningham Diary, 11 March 1946.

29. Cunningham Diary, 11 January 1946.

30. Cunningham Diary, 5 October 1945.

31. Owen (1945) p. 277.

32. Attlee Papers, Speech to Labour Party Demonstration in Leicester, 27 September 1947. See also his speech on receiving the freedom of the City of Birmingham, 18 October 1947.

33. Barclay (1975) p. 90.

34. Alexander Papers, Speech to American Legion at Chelsea Hospital, 9 September 1947.

35. Dalton Diary, 17 January 1947.

36. Owen (1945) p. 269.

37. Quoted in Conservative Political Centre (1950), Imperial Policy, June 1949.

38. Wyatt (1952) p. 236.

39. Attlee Papers, Speech at the Annual Banquet of the Birmingham Jewelers and Silversmiths Association, 23 March 1946.

40. Attlee Papers, Speech to Lobby Luncheon, 11 April 1946.

41. Parliamentary Debates, vol. 415, col. 1333, 7 November 1945.

42. Speech at the Guildhall, London, 15 May 1947, quoted in "George VI to his Peoples" (1952) p. 61.

43. Huizinga (1958) p. 86.

Part 4

The Evolution of Attitudes and Their Significance in Specific Areas of Foreign Policy

The Evolution of Attitudes and the Search For Prestige

In this final substantive section of the book, this brief chapter discusses the way in which attitudes towards foreign policy evolved during the early postwar years and the way in which those attitudes predisposed the policymakers to seek to maintain and indeed to create an illusory image of Britain's real world power situation. The following chapter focuses on certain specific issues in British foreign policy that arose during the period under review and considers the possible significance of attitudes in the decisions that were taken.

It should not be deduced from the synchronic nature of earlier chapters that the attitudes of the policymakers were static throughout the period under study. As the events of the early postwar years unfolded, there was some movement in attitudes towards the acceptance of a world role for Britain that was commensurate with her resources, but it was not in the least smooth or unidirectional; steps toward change would often be retraced; movement towards reduced intervention in one direction might be accompanied by movement towards increased intervention in another. Moreover, the speed at which attitudes evolved varied from one policymaker to another.

The growing perception of Britain's economic weakness and financial dependence on the United States, the failure to hold Palestine, the necessity of backing away from policy objectives in Greece and Turkey, and the expedited granting of Indian independence were events that must have undermined to some extent the more grandiose views of Britain's world role held at the end of the war. It will be remembered, however, that dissonance arising from contradictory cognitions or from differences between cognitive and affective attitudinal components can be dissipated in several ways; as the previous chapter made evident, the gradual acceptance that Britain could not afford to exercise the world role its leaders desired led to changes in attitudes at a cognitive level, but not to the same extent at an affective level. In matters of foreign policy, the *cognition* that Britain was a great power of the first order was weakened by the country's inability to get its way in several areas; however, the *feeling* that Britain was somehow an example to all nations and destined for enduring great power status was not noticeably weakened until the Suez crisis and the decolonization of the 1950s and, indeed, was still expressed in only slightly diminished form through the 1960s and beyond.[1] The strength of the policymakers' attitudes at an affective level influenced the process of attitudinal change at a cognitive level; when a cognition changed and became inconsistent with some affective component of an attitude, the ensuing dissonance-reducing mental activity would often result in the cognition reverting back to something near its original form as soon as there was some easing in the pressures that had caused the original change. It was this process that so infuriated Dalton--Ministers would accept his arguments for overseas retrenchment one week only to reject them or at least not press for any action to implement them some weeks later after the memory of his "scorching memo" had faded.

In short, attitudes towards Britain's world role at an affective level seem to have been almost stable over the period. The policymakers showed no readiness to contemplate Britain ever being anything less than a member of the great three powers, distinct in status from all other powers; there was no motivation to devise ways of withdrawing from imperial and other overseas commitments in the absence of compelling external pressures. At a cognitive level, on the other hand, there was a growing recognition that Britain would have to play a more modest role in the world than had first been envisaged, but this recognition grew jerkily because it involved creating an incongruity with the unchanging--or, at the very most, slowly changing--affective components of attitudes. It was this incongruity that led to the desperate effort to maintain the illusion of power and that explains so many of the contradictions in policy statements made by leaders of the time. Many of the paradoxes in foreign policy decision making during this period become easier to explain when the clash of attitudinal components and the natural human reaction of trying to minimize its emotional impact are taken into consideration.

THE SEARCH FOR PRESTIGE

The tension arising from the incongruity between the feeling that Britain should continue to play a world role of the first order and the cognition that her resources for doing so were clearly insufficient was relieved to some degree by the energies the policymakers exerted in efforts to win for Britain ever-increasing international prestige. Of course, most countries see the pursuit of international prestige as an essential foreign policy objective; however, in the case of Britain in the early postwar years, the authorities went beyond the task of presenting the country and its ideas in the best possible light and devoted considerable resources and energies to the maintenance of an image of world preeminence that far surpassed economic and strategic realities. In their minds, the discrepancy between the real power enjoyed after the Second World War would be less painful to acknowledge if other countries could be led to believe that Britain still retained her strategic capability and prowess, or at least to acknowledge that in matters political, social, and intellectual, Britain still provided an example worthy of emulation.

It was firmly believed that if Britain's prestige could be enhanced, the country could continue to exercise political power even though it would not be backed up by a matching strategic power. The more Britain's economic situation worsened, therefore, the more desperate became the search for international prestige. As Lord Templewood, a prewar Foreign Secretary, remarked at the time, "Our future more than ever depends on prestige rather than material wealth. Prestige is to nations what credit is to business. It is an asset that can be more powerful than material possessions."[2]

There were some voices in the earliest postwar years expressing concern at the search for an unjustified measure of prestige and recommending the adoption of a more modest foreign policy. The concern of Keynes and Dalton about the country insisting on "cutting a dash" in world affairs that went far beyond its resources has already been noted, and this concern was shared by a number of influential thinkers and particularly by publications of the political left. One expert on defence matters, G. R. Liddell Hart, warned of the dangers of Britain disregarding the natural limits of its strength and recommended a major reduction in Britain's overseas presence on the grounds that "a voluntary contraction, suitably timed, is less of a risk and forfeits less 'face' than an enforced retreat under hostile pressure."[3] *The New Statesman*, in a typical editorial in November 1947, attributed what it saw as Bevin's failures in Palestine, Germany, Iraq, and Greece to his measuring foreign policy by the yardstick of prestige rather than that of the country's actual strength.[4] However, for most policymakers the attitude that Britain's international prestige should be maintained if not enhanced was unassailably strong.

Seeking to maintain or enhance prestige was one of the major themes running through the Foreign Office files of the period. One of the clearest explanations of the reasons for the need to maintain prestige was formulated by an official serving in the embassy in Washington:

> I am convinced that if we can prove (a) that we are strong as
> a nation and as the centre of a great progressive
> Commonwealth and Empire, and (b) that, as part of that
> strength, we are becoming the moral and progressive leaders of
> the world, we have built the foundations of a greatly improved
> Anglo-American relationship, of greatly improved relations

with other countries, and of success at home. . . If we cannot
gain affection, we can at least win respect.[5]

Magill, attached to the Allied Control Commission to Finland, made a
parallel point with regard to Scandinavia and Russia:

> There are many Scandinavians who have swallowed the story
> that Britain is now a third class power. But this idea of our
> weakness and defeatism is one which we must at all costs
> eradicate from the minds of Scandinavians, since if the opinion
> once gained firm and widespread footing that we had written
> off Scandinavia to Russia, then all our efforts in the political
> and economic fields would be doomed to eventual failure.[6]

Both writers admit that Britain's world influence depended much more
on the skilful use of information and forceful propaganda than, for example, on
the strength of its fleet. Using such tactics became the main tasks of Britain's
Ambassadors, as Sir David Keely frankly admitted: "My main duty in Turkey,
1946 to 1948, was to maintain confidence in the value of the Anglo-Turkish
Alliance and to uphold British prestige during a period of economic and financial
difficulty."[7]

An amusing illustration of the degree to which officials were
preoccupied with the subject was provided in spring 1946, when Wardrop, the
British Ambassador to Norway, wrote to the Foreign Office with regard to the
forthcoming European Games:

> Sport, I need hardly say, plays a most important part in
> international relations and a country's prestige tends more and
> more on the success or otherwise of its teams when these go
> abroad. We very much hope, therefore, that if Great Britain
> is to be represented, the strongest available team will be sent
> over here. There is here, as elsewhere, quite a strong body of
> opinion which believes that the British are getting decadent and
> it would be fatal, therefore, to send out a sort of "B" team with
> the idea of "giving the other side a chance" rather than trying
> to run off with the maximum number of trophies. Every other
> country approaches these international games in a purely
> competitive spirit and I am afraid that, for the sake of prestige,
> we must follow suit.

On receipt of the communication at the Foreign Office, an official drafted a letter
to the Amateur Athletic Association: "Mr. Bevin hopes that it may be possible
to send a first class British team to the European games which could do much

to uphold Britain's prestige."[8]   Incidentally, his superior did not approve the transmittal on the grounds that the AAA might resent the implication that it normally sent less than first-class teams.

On the whole, the need for prestige was felt just as strongly among the political leaders. Attlee was very obviously torn between two conflicting sets of attitudes. He was never able to reconcile satisfactorily Dalton's demands for retrenchment on overseas expenditure with Bevin's demands for a strengthened British position in world affairs. As a capable economist himself, the Prime Minister could not deny the logic and validity of Dalton's observations; on the other hand, as a product of his age and education he could not bring himself to insist on any reductions in Britain's overseas role not made essential by the course of events in the external environment. This conflict explains why Attlee would often question the need for retention of certain British commitments at meetings of the Defence Committee but why, in spite of his authority, he would not insist on any cutbacks being made. For example, at a meeting of the Defence Committee in September 1945, Attlee backed Dalton against others who were arguing for a continued British presence in the West Indies: British troops, they claimed, were necessary there not for strategic reasons but because British prestige would suffer if the flag were not shown to the Americans in their home waters. The minutes of the meeting record that after Dalton had made a plea for cutting overseas expenditure as much as possible, Attlee proposed that garrison requirements in outlying areas should be carefully scrutinized and reduced to a minimum. Opposition to such views was fierce, particularly on the part of the military leaders. Having made his protest, Attlee backed down and the troops remained in the West Indies. However much he believed Dalton's reasoning, he could not bring himself to assume the responsibility for any loss of face abroad.[9]

Bevin, more fully immersed in foreign affairs, was convinced that if the British economy had been weakened by six years of war, then it was all the more important that public relations and propaganda should be employed to maintain British prestige and, in consequence, British influence in international fora. He was backed up in this conviction by other Cabinet members including even Aneurin Bevan, who placed on record his approval of Bevin's policies:

> The recent proceedings in the Security Council had enhanced
> British prestige in the eyes of the world, and the Cabinet were
> indebted to the Foreign Secretary for the skilful way in which
> he had handled these discussions.[10]

In short, despite warning voices, Bevin, the Cabinet, and the officials of the Foreign Office, unable to bring affective perceptions of Britain's world role in line with the economic and strategic realities of the postwar world, geared their policies towards sustaining an illusion of power. They believed that the more successful they were in achieving that objective, the more influence the country would retain in world affairs. They were predisposed, therefore, to build an illusion of power by retaining a British presence in as many places as possible, even though that might put pressure on the balance of payments and deprive the domestic economy of much-needed resources. When the illusion of power was first really challenged a decade after the end of the war, the country's inflated image burst like Aesop's frog. Sir Henry Tizard, chief scientist at the Ministry of Defence, had been both shrewd and prophetic when he had written in 1949:

> We persist in regarding ourselves as a great power capable of everything and only temporarily handicapped by economic difficulties. We are not a great power and never will be again. We are a great nation but if we continue to behave like a great power we shall soon cease to be a great nation. Let us take warning from the fate of the great powers of the past and not burst ourselves with pride.[11]

NOTES

1. Note, for example, that Harold Macmillan allegedly remarked at the time of Suez that if Britain failed to topple Nasser, it would become "another Netherlands". Harold Wilson soon after his election in 1964 said, "we are a world power and world influence or we are nothing". Quoted in Thorne (1978), p. 687.

2. Quoted in "United Empire" (1945), vol. 36, p. 141.

3. These ideas of G. R. Liddell Hart were expressed in his correspondence to Lord Hankey in March 1946; Hankey Papers, File HNKY 14/15.

4. New Statesman, 1 November 1947.

5. Attlee Papers, Correspondence from G. Mackenzie, 30 January 1946.

6. PRO, FO/371/47450, N15473/10928/G.63, 10 November 1945.

7. Kelly (1953) p. 337.

8. PRO, FO/371/56284, N4933/219/30, April 1946.

9. For another example of Attlee's attitudes on such matters, see Attlee Papers, Box 1, Letter to R. Mellish, 1 November 1946.

10. PRO, Cab 128/7, Cabinet Meeting 11 February 1946, Confidential Annexes.

11. Quoted by Professor M. Gowing in a public lecture at Leeds University reported in *The Times*, 11 October 1977, p. 4.

Attitudes and Specific
Policy Issues

Building on the general analysis of the formation and evolution of the attitudes of the policymakers, this chapter relates these attitudes to the decisions taken in the most important areas of British foreign policy in the early postwar years. Weighing the precise significance of attitudes in any particular decision would require a multifactorial analysis that would go beyond the framework of this book. However, the evidence presented in this chapter will demonstrate that the policymakers' attitudes wielded an influence in the decision-making process, which, even though not precisely quantified, cannot be ignored by those seeking to understand the events of the period.

THE EMPIRE

An understanding of the specific attitudes held with regard to the empire makes it easier to comprehend perceptions of Britain's role in wider international affairs. Attlee and his government inherited a vast overseas empire that had been put together over a period of more than 400 years. In 1945 the British Empire covered more than one-quarter of the world's land surface and a similar proportion of its population. By this time its membership was no longer homogenous; Canada had achieved virtual independence under the Crown in 1867, and this "dominion" status, as it was later to be termed, had been won subsequently by Australia, New Zealand, and South Africa. The dominions retained allegiance to the Crown but could make foreign policy decisions independently, as indeed had been made evident at the beginning of the Second

World War. The rest of the empire was made up of India and of numerous colonies won for the Crown by British adventurers and of the protectorates placed under British control by various international bodies. Added to these countries in many British minds were those countries such as Egypt and Iraq that were linked to Britain by major defence treaties. By the terms of the 1931 Statute of Westminster, all units of the empire were to work towards self-government and to become independent states within the British Commonwealth of Nations. Despite this statute and despite the very different status of all the countries involved, most British people still perceived of the empire as a single entity. It was that part of the world map that was coloured pink, from Canada in the top left-hand corner ranging across Africa and India to Australia and New Zealand in the bottom right-hand corner. As has already been noted several times, the existence of so much pink-coloured territory was a source of immense pride and satisfaction.

Pride in the empire was probably proclaimed most stridently by Conservative politicians. Churchill, obviously concerned that the integrity of the British Empire would be undermined in the period following the war, warned the Foreign Office:

> There must be no question of being hustled or seduced into declarations affecting British sovereignty in any of the dominions or colonies. Pray remember my declaration against liquidating the British Empire. . . "Hands off the British Empire" is our maxim and it must not be weakened or smirched to please sob-stuff merchants at home or foreigners of any hue.[1]

To which the Foreign Office rather indignantly replied: "there is not the slightest question of liquidating the British Empire." Churchill's concern that the concept of the British Empire was being attacked from abroad was probably motivated mainly by the crude antiBritish Empire feelings, relics of the country's colonial past, that had surfaced in the United States and by those commentators who predicted that the United States would not be challenged in its world power preeminence by the British Empire, but, on the contrary, would ultimately be forced to defend it.[2]

As to the "sob-stuff merchants at home," many Tory speakers cast Labour politicians in this role. One Tory M.P., for example, claimed that the socialist government had failed because it was "fundamentally international and so philosophically opposed to the British Empire and historically ashamed of its glorious achievements."[3] These remarks might well have applied to the small number of Marxist intellectuals within the British Labour movement but could not have been applied at all to the Cabinet or to the vast majority of Labour Party members, whose socialism was based far more on the motivation to bring about humanitarian reforms than on deep reading of Karl Marx or other socialist philosophers. During their period in opposition, Labour MPs had criticized Tory imperial policies and the concept of imperialism in general. Hobson's analysis of the exploitative nature of imperialism, first published in 1902, had exerted an undeniable influence on Labour Party thinking.[4] However, being opposed to the exploitation of one country by another did not mean being opposed to the British Empire in any form. On the contrary, the majority of the Labour Party saw the empire as a "sacred trust" of civilization to be honorably discharged and not a disgraceful burden to be jettisoned. In the same speech a British socialist could call for independence for the colonies and for greater intervention in those colonies by the British Government. No paradox was implied because helping a country to avoid tribal wars and to build up its economy in preparation for independence corresponded ideally with the predominant humanitarian reformist school of thought within the Labour movement. Even though Britain might have exploited its empire in the past, Labour politicians did not believe that the country could undo that evil simply by withdrawing from the scene of the crime; there was still a debt to history waiting to be discharged.[5]

Labour politicians spoke more often of the commonwealth than the empire, unlike their Conservative counterparts. They were also more likely to call forcefully for progress towards independence. The difference between the two parties was, however, more semantic than real. In practice the concept of empire held by the two parties was virtually identical. No Conservative leaders could have taken issue with the Labour colonial philosophy as expressed by Arthur Creech Jones, Secretary of State for the Colonies between 1946 and 1950:

> Much of what is wrong in underdeveloped societies comes because of the poverty of nature and backwardness of people who have been insulated for centuries and tied by tradition and tribalism and oppressed by ignorance and superstition. It is not due to rapacious capitalism or modern exploiting "Colonialism," tragic and appalling as have been many instances of cruelty and exploitation and interventions from outside.

There should be no question, he continued, "of abdication of Britain from obligations incurred in the past, or of transfers of territories to inexperienced or to some non-existent international authority. . . Democratic government in the hands of ignorant and politically inexperienced people can easily become unworkable. It is exposed to mass emotional appeals; mass ignorance and prejudice can be exploited."[6] Herbert Morrison remarked in a similar vein:

> It would be ignorant, dangerous nonsense to talk about grants of full self-government to many of the dependent territories for

some time to come. In those instances it would be like giving
a child of ten a latch key, a bank account and a shot gun.[7]

No Conservative politician could have spoken in a more paternal manner.
Despite Tory accusations to the contrary, the Labour government was committed
to a continuation and a strengthening of the British Empire. The opposition to
the empire expressed by some socialist intellectuals and by foreign commentators
served only to reinforce the pro-imperial attitudes of the Cabinet and of other
policymakers.

Pro-imperial attitudes among Cabinet members existed at a cognitive
level but perhaps more profoundly at an affective level. General feelings toward
the empire were characterized by pride and satisfaction. Attlee often became
emotional about the empire. It was a "living organism with a marvelous power
of adaptation to new circumstances and conditions,"[8] a peculiarly British
phenomenon, a group of cricket-playing countries whose unity and success could
not be understood by foreigners.[9] At the height of Britain's economic problems
he obviously took great satisfaction in praising the British people for their
continued commitment "to extend freedom and democracy throughout the empire
and to develop one of the greatest political ventures of all time, the British
Commonwealth of Nations."[10]

Bevin's emotional attachment to the empire was no less great. Well
before his entry into government he had told the Trades Union Congress:

> We have been left the. . . responsibility of an empire and we
> will not break it up, we will not destroy it. It is at least a third
> of the world linked together in various forms. Instead of
> breaking it up we will carry it a stage further forward by using
> an economic organization that we can create through the
> League and from Empire Organization we will pass into the
> stage of world organization.[11]

The way Bevin's attachment to the empire affected his conduct as
Foreign Secretary is well illustrated by an anecdote, probably substantially true,
recounted by a correspondent of *The Times*, Iverach Macdonald:

> When a string of Ambassadors were calling upon him in turn
> to offer the usual politenesses, he received the Guatemalan
> head of mission. Listening rather abstractedly. . . he became
> aware that the envoy seemed to be not just uttering platitudes
> but to be putting forward some sort of claim to British
> Honduras. . . In great perplexity he asked, "*What* country did
> you say you represent? I see. And now you want a bit of the

British Empire?" He gazed at the envoy in complete and sincere bewilderment. "But you must have *known* the answer would be No."[12]

Cripps, who was often accused by the Tories of being against the empire,[13] dispelled any doubts on this score by a number of speeches in 1945 and after; for example, in a pre-election broadcast, he told his audience, "Our country and our Commonwealth must be powerful and strong because we want to be able to give leadership to the world towards greater peace and prosperity."[14]

Other members of the Cabinet demonstrated a similar attachment to the concept of empire. Alexander spoke of the "stout old British Empire ship" that needed bringing "safely through another storm";[15] Morrison declared that he was a friend of the "Jolly old Empire" and was going "to stick to it";[16] Dalton was opposed to the development of closer political links with Europe, preferring his vision of a "British Socialist Commonwealth."[17] Other government Ministers saw the extension of their plans for Britain throughout the empire and commonwealth. "For us," John Strachey explained, "it is not a question of socialism in one country--it is a question of socialism in one Commonwealth."[18] The unity between the political right and the broad left is well summed up by Shinwell's description of his first meeting with Conservative newspaper proprietor Lord Beaverbrook in 1945: "we both believed in the empire but disagreed on almost every detail in our creed."[19]

In short, policymakers evidenced a general, deeply held attachment to the British Empire. In their eyes the empire was the most tangible evidence of British greatness, and to cast doubts on it would have necessitated a rejection of all the attitudes concerning British superiority that had been learned at school and reinforced over and over again by the prevailing intellectual climate. In the words of one contemporary writer: "The empire stands for the common tradition of the British people, its aspirations and achievements. It symbolizes above all the greatness of the nation and its contribution to civilization."[20]

The degree to which the empire was seen to be an integral part of Britain is made apparent by the serious consideration that was given to the possibility of dispersing the British population throughout the Commonwealth for both strategic and economic reasons. This subject was discussed at the Commonwealth Prime Ministers meeting in 1946, on the basis of a paper prepared by the Chiefs of Staff.[21] Certainly, Army Chief of Staff Alanbrooke together with Sir Henry Tizard both spoke out for the transfer of as much British manpower and industry as possible to the dominions, seeing it as an essential means of overcoming British vulnerability in the approaching nuclear era.[22] The issue was given serious consideration in navy circles as well, as a letter to

Lord Hankey in 1947 from the Royal Navy's Deputy Controller of Research and Development revealed:

> For three years I have been preaching that the solution lies in distributing ourselves and our resources throughout the Commonwealth and I have not changed my mind. It might take 50 years or more to do and I feel that somehow or other we have to keep out of war until the redistribution is effected. . . . the Pax Britannica once worked and a Pax Atomerica, though unpalatable, might give us the time for redistribution.[23]

No specific action seems to have been taken on these ideas, but the fact that they can have been considered as seriously as they were indicates how the empire was seen as an integrated whole and as part and parcel of the British experience. The immediate post-Second World War years were the last in which such notions could be firmly held; as decolonization gathered pace in the 1950s and as, in consequence, the political and intellectual climate changed, plans for juggling population around from one part of a united empire to another would have seemed increasingly absurd.

In the period directly following the war, the idea was often expressed that the empire should serve as a model for any future world organization. The empire and commonwealth represented a group of widely disparate countries that had cooperated peacefully together; logically, if other countries could forge similar relationships, world peace would be assured. Both Attlee and Bevin made this point frequently in speaking about the establishment of a United Nations Organization and other international organizations.[24]

However, not only was the British Empire seen as providing a model for the world to follow, it was also seen as providing Britain with a source of real power. After all, potential strength in terms of real resources, manpower, and diplomatic and technical experience was at least as great in the empire as in America and Russia combined. It was partly because of this fact that voices pointing to the indiscriminate maintenance of imperial commitments as a source of British weakness were given so little credence. The Conservatives were particularly forthright in declaring the empire as a source of British power and in pamphlet warned of the dire consequences of failing to maintain it intact: "We believe that if the British Empire were to break up Britain would become a third class power, unable to feed or defend herself."[25] Attitudes held by Labour government Ministers were similar. According to Francis Williams, one of Attlee's closest advisers, the policymakers saw the immediate aftermath of the war as "a moment. . . when Britain's continued existence as a world power was more dependent than at any time in her history upon her ability to remain in the centre of a World Commonwealth of associated and friendly nations."[26] Bevin had spoken of the need for a tightly organized imperial federation acting as a world power bloc since at least the 1920s.[27]   At the Foreign Office it was evident that he was still dazzled by the vision of the potential of the empire for increasing Britain's world power. As he told Dalton, "If we only pushed on and developed Africa, we could have U.S. dependent on us, and eating out of our hand, in 4 or 5 years."[28]   One of Bevin's objectives as Foreign Secretary was to strengthen the empire and commonwealth and to link them in some way with a closely-knit Western Europe to form a powerful and British-dominated, Eurocentric system that would enable Britain to talk on at least equal terms with the new super-powers.

The attitudes of the political leaders were not in conflict with those of the bureaucracy that served them. Lord Franks saw Britain's relationship with the empire and commonwealth as:

> the relationship which enables us to play in the big league with the continental powers. It is success here which permits us to stand out of the queue and fill the role of a great power, which gives us reasonable independence among our friends and a part in the great decisions. This is why it is vital that we see the Commonwealth and Britain's job in it as clearly as we can.[29]

The military leaders, remembering the significant contribution made by some parts of the empire during the war, were unanimous in their view of the empire and commonwealth as a source of British power. Army Chief of Staff Lord Alanbrooke reflected their attitudes when he argued that "the maintenance of peace in this world depends on the solidarity of our commonwealth more than on any other factor."[30]   Prevailing attitudes were perhaps best summed up in the report of a Royal Institute of International Affairs research group. The links with the empire and commonwealth, it argued, "are great responsibilities and charges upon British energy, but they are also great supports of British strength."[31]

Feelings that the wellbeing of the British Empire was a symbol of the progress and superiority of the British people, that it provided a model for international relations and peaceful coexistence, and that it was a source of political and strategic strength for Britain obviously did not predispose the policymakers to seek actively to reduce their country's role as an imperial power; on the contrary, such feelings made them wish to strengthen and enhance it. Obviously there were a number of other factors that serve to explain the position the country took with regard to the empire. Although the cost to the British taxpayer of administering and developing the colonies rose from just under £9 million in 1944-45 to just over £13 million in 1945-46 and to over £26 million in 1946-47,[32] the empire did bring significant economic benefits. In the dollar shortage that followed the war, a number of colonies such as Malaya were dollar earners, and many of them sold Britain goods for sterling that could only have been obtained elsewhere for dollars. There were also legal obligations to the empire that the British policymakers could not ignore; for example, a large proportion of the £3,355 million liabilities with which Britain was left at the end of the war was owed to members of the empire that had made loans and provided services during the hostilities. There was also the commitment to spend some £120 million over ten years enshrined in the Colonial Development and Welfare Act passed in 1945 with the backing of Attlee and Bevin as members of the coalition Cabinet.

But these factors alone cannot be used to justify some of the decisions that were taken in imperial matters. For example, Sarawak was accepted as a new British colony even though the native representatives on the Sarawak Legislative Council were opposed to the cession and even though there was no prospect of Britain deriving any financial gain. In the Lord Chancellor's view, Britain's decision to accept Sarawak as a new colony was motivated by the "sole desire. . . to inaugurate some system which will improve the conditions of life of the inhabitants of Sarawak and to bring the administration of the territory at least up to the level of that obtaining in other comparable colonial territories."[33]

The Sarawak incident and the strong arguments advanced by some Ministers and officials for Britain to assume responsibility for the former Italian colonies in North Africa should not be used as evidence of a resurgence of a Disraelian desire to expand the empire yet further, but they are evidence that thoughts turned more easily to some expansion rather than any contraction of the imperial responsibility. If anything, the Second World War had helped to revive Britain's sense of imperial responsibility. Whatever policymakers perceived at a cognitive level, at an affective level they had a strengthened commitment to the continuation of the country's imperial role. The way in which feelings overpowered cognitions is well illustrated in a statement by the Secretary of the Fabian Colonial Research Bureau who wrote towards the end of the war:

> I was a rabid anti-imperialist at one time, but one cannot ignore the fact that there is a certain sympathy, an intangible something, which holds the British Commonwealth or Empire together and which cannot be wholly explained in terms of material advantage.[34]

THE WITHDRAWAL FROM INDIA

One major event in British imperial history that occurred during the term of office of Attlee's Cabinet--the granting of independence to India--may at first sight seem to contradict what has just been said. Surely, the British withdrawal from the country that had been seen as the very centre of the empire must have necessitated a massive change in traditional attitudes. Did not Britain's willingness to leave India compare most favorably with, for example, France's intransigence with regard to Indochina and Algeria? To answer these questions it is necessary to look briefly at the background to the events leading up to the handing over of power.

While most of the early British leaders in India saw their objective as starting the process of preparing the Indian people to use British-style democratic institutions so that at some future time they would be able to assume the government of their own country, as time went by and as the strategic value of India increased, the focus of the imperial administrators turned to the indefinite extension of British rule. The vision of the "noblest" or the "proudest" day when Britain would withdraw, her work accomplished, faded from sight. Lord Curzon, who was Viceroy of India around the turn of the century, in fact ordered the removal of "Onward Christian Soldiers" from the order of service in Delhi's Red Fort because of its allusion to the impermanence of earthly empires--"Crowns and Thrones may perish, Kingdoms rise and wane."[35]

From the time of Lord Curzon until the end of the Second World War, the demands for Indian independence became increasingly vocal and widespread, and what concessions different British governments made to weaken pro-independence groups by granting concessions generally served only to increase frustrations. In fact, the disappointment at the terms of postwar independence offered by Cripps on behalf of the British wartime Cabinet in 1942 led directly to the birth of the "Quit India" movement. After the end of the war in Europe, the Viceroy, Lord Wavell, called a conference in Simla between the leading Indian politicians, including the leaders of the Congress whom he had just released from prison, where they had been sent for their encouragement of the 'Quit India' movement. This conference was marked by bitter arguments among the Indian delegates, but it confirmed in their minds the fact that Britain was prepared to withdraw and cede to them the government of their country. The atmosphere at this time was tense. The Congress leaders pursued the goal of a united Indian nation with an energy that had been pent up during their months in prison; the Moslem League sought the creation of Pakistan, an independent Moslem state, with equal vigour; and various other groups, including an emerging communist movement, clamoured for their own concept of India free from British rule. Students rioted, sailors mutinied, and politicians delivered provocative speeches; it was in this atmosphere that the Labour Government came into power in 1945.

In spite of these very obvious tensions, many in Britain--including notably Winston Churchill--still believed that a British presence of some sort in India could and should continue after the war. They were motivated not only by the need to maintain the strategic advantages that bases in India gave but also often by a romantic attraction to the benevolent British Raj that they saw as benefiting the majority of the Indian population. For the Attlee Government, however, there was never really any choice as to whether or not India should be granted full independence, only how and when. The political situation in India was such that any reluctance on the British side to proceed rapidly towards full independence would have provoked unrest and rebellion that for its containment would have required a major military effort that the Government would not have been able to mount without reneging on defence commitments elsewhere in the world or cutting back on the flow of demobilized servicemen and imports to British industry that was desperate for both. Moreover, the granting of independence to India was being requested by Britain's needed ally, the United States;[36] it had been an article of faith of the Labour Party in opposition; and it had been promised by many Labour MPs in their election manifestos.[37] In consequence, any attempts to maintain Britain's power in India could have provoked serious national and international political problems. Therefore, even though Bevin would have liked to have seen the continuation of at least some British influence in India, he was forced to agree with Attlee that the realities of the situation demanded a withdrawal, more or less on terms laid down by the Indian leaders. Both they and other Cabinet members were unanimous, however, in believing that it would have to be presented as a gesture of strength and moral responsibility rather than as an accommodation to exogenous pressures. The minutes of the Cabinet meetings between the Labour Government's entry into power in the summer of 1945 and the final granting of independence to India and Pakistan in 1947 show considerable concern that the withdrawal from India should be effected in a manner that would do the least harm to Britain's image. Ministers were anxious that Britain should maintain her world status and prestige while accepting a course of events that in real terms could only represent a loss of power and authority.

In June 1946, the problems with India seemed overwhelming. A Cabinet mission composed of Pethick Lawrence, Cripps, and Alexander had returned from India having had no success in bridging the widening gap between the Moslem League and the Congress. In their meeting of June 5, the Cabinet expressed a preference for maintaining British rule "until the Indians were able to agree on a plan," but the Ministers agreed, if such a course "evoked widespread resistance, the policy would have to be modified, if only because it would involve very substantial reinforcement of our troops which we should have great difficulty in finding."[38] Clearly the Ministers remained concerned that Britain's international status should not be weakened. The Cabinet, no doubt recalling the political capital Churchill had extracted from what he had termed the "scuttle" withdrawal from Burma a few months before,

> took the view that having regard to current difficulties in Palestine and Egypt, it was important to avoid any course which could be represented as a policy of "scuttle." This would provoke very strong reactions in this country and in the

Dominions and would have a most damaging effect on our international position. . . we must at all costs avoid a situation in which we had to withdraw from India under circumstances of ignomy.[39]

A few days later Bevin issued a Cabinet paper on India drafted for him by his Foreign Office officials:

In general, any action by His Majesty's Government which appears to suggest that we are abandoning our position in India. . . would weaken our position in international affairs to the extent that it can be interpreted as evidence of a decline in British power and resolution.

The Foreign Office was particularly anxious to maintain face vis-à-vis the Americans; they should not be led to believe "that we no longer had the means to face our responsibilities." There was also concern about Britain's reputation in other parts of the world: "Any apparent weakness on our part will adversely affect our prestige throughout the Far East and correspondingly diminish our influence and authority."[40] These attitudes towards Indian affairs are typical of those expressed in other Cabinet papers and discussions during the period leading up to independence.

It cannot be denied that together with Lord Mountbatten, the last Viceroy in India, the Attlee Cabinet's handling of the Indian question deserves commendation: responsible efforts were made to ensure a peaceful transition of power and the withdrawal took place as soon as it became clear that a British presence could no longer be useful in the climate that then existed. It must not be forgotten, however, that in spite of views to the contrary expressed by some Conservative and by some military leaders, Britain had no choice but to leave India quickly after the war.[41] Her withdrawal in summer 1947 was followed by much bloodshed but almost certainly not as much as would have followed attempts to prolong British power by force of arms, a course of action it would have been practically impossible to follow.

The control of India had been for decades the foundation of Britain's status as the world's greatest imperial power. Even though India was to remain a member of the commonwealth, Britain, in losing direct control and in allowing that foundation to be removed, lost elements of her real power position. Of all the components of the constellation of attitudes concerning the Indian question, certainly one of the most important was the concern that the loss of real power should be disguised. Hopes were indeed expressed that the world would be so impressed with Britain's magnanimous gesture granted from a position of strength that British influence and prestige in the postwar world would perhaps even be increased.

In summary, both Cabinet Ministers and civil service leaders concerned with foreign and imperial affairs were agreed that the empire was a source of strength for Britain and that it provided a model of international cooperation worthy of emulation. The fact that the Labour Ministers placed more emphasis on Britain's moral responsibility to bring progress and development to the colonies does not alter the fact that, at an affective level, they shared the Conservatives' pride at the country's imperial role, a pride that was an integral component of their view of Britain as a preeminent world power. With the exception of India and Burma, where events forced their hand, the policymakers gave no serious consideration to cutting back on overseas imperial commitments as a means of strengthening the domestic economy. The withdrawal from the heart of the empire was not the first step in a socialist plan to give independence to all the colonies as soon as possible but was rather more an unavoidable bowing before nationalistic pressures that were stronger and potentially more powerful than those already stirring in other parts of the British and other European empires. The discussions preceding this event provide evidence that in this case there was a shift in cognitions that was strong enough to overwhelm the unchanged affective components of the traditional attitudes towards Britain's role in the world.

THE UNITED STATES, THE SOVIET UNION, AND THE UNITED NATIONS

The frequency and scope of contacts between the British and the United States authorities increased significantly in the years following the close of the Second World War. Long discussions were held between them about peace treaties and all the complex aspects of a postwar settlement with the Axis powers. In addition, as the months passed by, increasing amounts of time were given to the analysis of ways to overcome the threat that was seen to be posed to world peace by the Soviet Union, the two countries' former ally. There were also frequent meetings and negotiations concerning matters of bilateral interest, such as Britain's need for dollar loans to shore up her weakened economy. In fact, during those years, there were very few areas of foreign policy that were not the subject of consultation with the United States.

Several components of the British attitude towards the United States changed over the period under study. Optimism that the alliance that had won such great victories would function harmoniously after the war's end was soon dissipated by, among other things, the abrupt termination of the Lend-Lease programme and by stiff conditions attached to the U.S. loan to Britain--many felt it should have been free not only of conditions but also of interest in recognition of the fact that many of Britain's economic problems originated from her lone stand in defence of democracy. Pessimism over the loan and over fears that the United States would withdraw once again into isolation was in turn dissipated in later months as the European Recovery Programme was instigated and as the long-term involvement of United States troops in Europe was confirmed. It is interesting to note, however, that whatever changes in perception were taking place at political, strategic, and economic levels, British policymakers continued to feel that at moral and intellectual levels Britain remained superior to the United States. The existence of such paternalistic feelings provides another reason why the British policymakers were so reluctant to cede any elements of great power status and particularly to consider reductions in British overseas interests.

Feelings of paternalism with regard to the United States were most apparent among officials at the Foreign Office, where there was a general belief that Britain should take the initiative in defining the most appropriate goals in international affairs. Reacting to hostile comments in the American press about Britain's European policy, one official, H. O. Clarke, wrote, "If we are not prepared to act in Europe as we think right and give a lead to America in view of our greater experience, we shall forfeit not only our own self-respect but their respect for us."[42]

The policymakers' fear that the United States might draw back once again into isolation was based not only on recollections of isolationist sentiments expressed by a number of U.S. statesmen and politicians but also by the belief that the American people were basically immature and lacked Britain's experience and shrewdness of vision in dealing with international affairs. Another Foreign Office official, J. C. Donnelly, welcomed the signs of America's emergence from isolation and her plans to expand her diplomatic and economic activity to the level made feasible by the growth of her material power, but asked with some concern:

> To what extent will this foreign policy be successfully implemented? Despite many signs of greater maturity, American opinion and endeavours may still not prove able to maintain the equilibrium and unity which such a policy will inevitably require. . . I fear that it is not at all a foregone conclusion that this immense machine. . . will prove able to deal in an intelligent and consistent manner with the problems which face it once peace returns.[43]

Certainly the leading American diplomats were not seen to be on a par with their British counterparts. Speaking of Harry Hopkins one official warned, "allowance must be made in such envoys for lack of experience in the technique of diplomacy."[44] For the Foreign Office, it was clear that Britain was not and should not be considered as a subordinate of the United States. In a common phrase of the time, it was the United States that had all the money and Britain that had all the brains. Attlee's views were identical with those of the Foreign

Office. He once told Chuter-Ede that Britain was "engaged in negotiations with two nations who were far from being swayed by idealism--Russia and America. Both were very immature nations."[45]

There is nothing to suggest that Herbert Morrison changed his impression of America gained during his visit immediately before the war. America, he maintained, was 50 to 100 years behind Britain in social legislation, about 50 years behind in housing, and about 30 years on labour legislation.[46] Bevin did not portray the same superciliousness or sense of superiority towards the Americans that was shown by many of his colleagues; it is nevertheless obvious that he devoted much energy to persuading America to strengthen and protect British interests without giving the impression that Britain was weakening. For example, one of his principal reasons for opposing any referral to the United Nations of the Indian problem was his concern that the United States should not be led to believe "that we no longer had the means or resolution to face our responsibilities."[47]

The fact that Bevin and others so actively sought American help and cooperation cannot be taken as evidence of any desire to reduce the sphere of British overseas interests; on the contrary, American resources and strategic strength were sought above all to reinforce and defend Great Britain and her commonwealth. There was a strong desire that dependence on American strength in strategic matters should not be transformed into general subordination. As Attlee recalled, "we had to hold up our position vis-à-vis the Americans. We could not allow ourselves to be wholly in their hands."[48]   In short, the policymakers as a body perceived the need for close Anglo-American relationships not so much to compensate for Britain's new weakness as to enhance her old strength.

A similar analysis of British relations with the Soviet Union also sheds light on the policymakers' reluctance to consider cutting back on British overseas interests and accepting a more modest world role in the interests of building up the national economy.   What hopes were held of harmonious peacetime collaboration with the Soviet Union at the end of the war were soon dissipated. Soviet intransigence at the conference tables and consolidation of power in captured territory in Eastern Europe rapidly convinced both political and Foreign Office leaders that the fears of the Soviet leaders' imperialistic designs, which they had often voiced following the successful Soviet counterattacks during the war, were well justified.

At Potsdam, the possibility that the Soviet Union would go along with the British view of the postwar settlement was entertained, although the worst was assumed. As Dixon wrote at the time:

> Debate on the perennial question whether Russia is peaceful
> and wants to join the Western Club but is suspicious of us, or

whether she is out to dominate the world and is hoodwinking us. It always seems safer to go on the worse assumption.[49]

After Potsdam, few believed anymore that the Soviet Union wanted to join or even cooperate with the Western Club, and the policymakers became more determined than before to contain Soviet expansionism as much as possible. Maintaining a widespread British presence overseas became acknowledged as one means of achieving that end. Any withdrawal from positions overseas, it was feared, would create a "vacuum" into which the Russians would flow. In recalling how his government had felt the responsibility to maintain world peace, Attlee explained:

> It was essential to avoid reducing British commitments in such a way as to create power vacuums out of which might come new conflicts. . . which might tempt the Soviet Union to strike out for domination over the whole of Europe and the Middle East and thus divide the world beyond hope of repair.[50]

This fear of a vacuum was often echoed by Bevin[51] and by Alexander, who accused the Soviets of wanting the "gradual submersion" of the British Commonwealth.[52] The fear of Soviet expansionist designs was often used to justify the retention of a British presence not only in Europe but also in all parts of the world, from the Middle East to Latin America. For example, Bevin made clear his feeling that it was one of the essential reasons for Britain retaining its presence in Greece. In a memorandum to the Defence Committee, he wrote:

> If the Russian challenge to our position in Greece and Turkey is successfully countered in its early stages, it is probable that the Soviet Government will not persevere in their present policy. But if they are successful in Greece, Turkey would be the next to go and an assault on our position in the Middle East would soon follow. The one thing that might encourage them to persevere in their present course would be for us to weaken in our determination to preserve Greece.[53]

Defending Greece from Russian expansionism can be seen as an appropriate foreign policy action. What was inappropriate in the circumstances of the time, however, was the lack of really serious efforts to get other noncommunist powers to share the burden of this defence. It was only when Dalton and the Treasury took a firm line and stated that it was simply impossible to find significant new resources for an expansion of the British presence in Greece that Bevin took serious steps towards such burden-sharing. In early 1947, Bevin informed the Americans that unless they chose to intervene more actively, the anticommunist campaign in Greece and Turkey might fail. The telegram conveying this information has become famous; for many it was the positive response of the United States to Bevin's plea that marked the real beginning of the Cold War. In fact, there is some uncertainty surrounding the events leading up to the expedition of the telegram. Some see its expedition as one of Bevin's master strokes of foreign policy, timed precisely to get the desired American response.[54] Dalton, however, suggests the telegram was basically a draft by the Treasury that Bevin signed rather unwillingly in a moment of acute indisposition after mounting several flights of stairs to attend a Cabinet meeting in Great George Street during one of the frequent power cuts of winter 1947.[55] Dalton's diary entries may well have been distorted by his evident egocentricity, but it is nevertheless certain that the failure to increase British spending in Greece came about more because of Treasury intransigence than of any policy reappraisal by the Foreign Office.

The political leaders' conviction that Britain had responsibilities to contain Soviet expansionism with the help, if possible, of America and other allies was shared by leaders of both the Foreign Office and the armed services. Sir Maurice Petersen, who was appointed British Ambassador in Moscow in 1946, wrote of his belief in:

> the principle that nature abhors a vacuum. . . there was a vacuum in the Balkans and it was only natural that it should in part be filled by the Soviet Union. . . if a vacuum once existed in the Levant states, stability in other parts of the Middle East might well be affected.[56]

The Foreign Office Research Department's Handbook on "British Policy in Latin America" remarked that "the elimination of Britain from the Latin American scene would not mean that the United States would become the heir to everything Britain lost in the way of commerce and prestige" but would lead to a vacuum and, even in that part of the world, to possible Russian intervention.[57]

A paper emanating from the British element of the Allied Control Commission to Finland recommended that Britain adopt a coordinated policy towards Scandinavia designed "to prevent the complete domination of the whole of Scandinavia by Russia. . . if Scandinavia is divided and unsupported by the West, the vacuum will be filled from the East." The Nordic people had to be impressed, he continued, that "we do not propose to let Scandinavia slide unresisting into the jaws of Russia and that second, with cooperation from the Scandinavian side, we have the power as well as the will to prevent this happening."[58]

Although the Foreign Office officials who reviewed this paper found it amateurish and perhaps premature in its views of Soviet designs on Scandinavia, they did not refute its suggestions. Montgomery's agitation for a postwar continental strategy sprung directly from his belief that Britain should exercise responsibility for containing Soviet expansionism.[59]   Navy Chief of Staff Cunningham tended to equate any reduction in British overseas commitments as a capitulation to Moscow.   He noted in his diary of 12 July 1945, "Much discussion on a paper on 'security of the British Empire' by the Post-war Planners. A very pusillanimous document which talked mostly about retreat before the Russians."[60]

In short, the leaders of the Cabinet, the Foreign Office, and the military were united in feeling that British withdrawal from overseas commitments, almost anywhere in the world, could serve to encourage Soviet expansionism.

At the end of the war there was a widespread assumption that the new United Nations Organization would assume an important world peace-keeping role. Attlee had, after all, told the UN Assembly that "It is the firm intention of His Majesty's Government to make the success of the United Nations the primary object of their foreign policy: the security of the British Empire and Commonwealth is bound up with the success of the United Nations."[61] As late as December 1946, he wrote in one Labour Party publication that government foreign policy was "to make the United Nations and its charter the overriding factor in international affairs."[62] Many similar professions of faith were made by his Cabinet colleagues. Bevin, for example, in his election address, explained the major thrust of his foreign policy: "I stand for the World Security Organization, to prevent any more of these terrible wars."[63]

Here once again, however, it seems that early optimism was rapidly dissipated. The policymakers soon took the position that the United Nations would be unable to relieve Britain of any of her responsibilities as long as the Soviet Union was a key member with a right of veto or, of even more concern, with a right to include its own troops in any international peacekeeping force. In the case of India, for example, Bevin implored the Cabinet not to involve the UN in any way. If the UN was asked to restore order in India, he said, "the Soviet Union would be the only country, which would be both ready and able to supply the necessary number of troops. The result of such an appeal might therefore amount in practice to handing over the empire of India to the Soviet Union."[64]

Even without the wariness about the Soviet Union, it seems unlikely that Britain would have used the UN as a means of shedding overseas responsibilities. Britain would have tried to use the UN to supplement and strengthen its world role and would not have used it in any process of retreat from world power. Britain was still too proud to submit to any supranational authority and would only willingly have supported the UN to the extent that its decisions conformed with the intent of British policy.

In conclusion, in studying British relations with the United States, with the Soviet Union, and with the United Nations, it is evident that the British policymakers feared greatly that their country could be assigned to the second tier of world powers. This fear fed the reluctance to reduce overseas commitments and the desire to conjure up if not the substance at least the illusion of continuing first-tier status.

THE ATOM BOMB

A study of the debate between the policymakers regarding the development of a British atomic bomb in the immediate postwar years reveals several expressions of the attitude that Britain should continue to play the role of a first- rather than of a second-tier world power. Obviously so sensitive a subject was not publicly debated at the time, and what files have been made accessible on "tube alloys"--the official euphemism used for several years for atomic questions--are not comprehensive. However, the evidence available from public records together with the recollections of officials involved, if not revealing every precise detail of the decision-making process, do at least point to certain basic attitudes that influenced the policymakers as they weighed the questions involved.

The first use of atomic bombs in Japan made a great impression on Britain's military leaders. At a time when the use of strategic bombing was seen as an essential, and even the most essential, component of the conduct of war, the atomic bomb seemed to be the superlative weapon. It was commonly accepted then that the bombs that had fallen on Hiroshima and Nagasaki had shortened the war with Japan by some six months or more and had saved thousands of lives among the American and allied forces. It seemed obvious in the aftermath of the explosions that atomic bombs wreaked such terrible damage that their very existence could serve as a deterrent to future wars.

The military leaders had no desire to relive the frustrations of the early 1930s when they had been prevented from pursuing national interests because of the country's lack of a sufficient margin of superiority in men and weaponry over her adversary. The Chiefs of Staff became anxious that atomic bombs should be added to the country's arsenal as soon as possible, and they recommended in October 1945 that British production of such weapons should start right away, warning that "to delay production pending the outcome of negotiations regarding international control might well prove fatal to the security of the British Commonwealth."[65] Bevin shared their impatience; he had no time for the American-inspired Baruch plan for international control and is reported to have said, "Let's forget about the 'Baroosh' and get on with making the 'fissle'."[66]

At first, the hope was that the production of the British bomb would result from a continuation of wartime Anglo-American cooperation. British scientists had played a prominent part in the design and development of the first bomb, and the aide-memoire signed by Roosevelt and Churchill at Hyde Park in

September 1944 provided that the development of atomic energy should continue after the defeat of Japan unless and until terminated by joint agreement. Two days after the Hiroshima explosion, Attlee wrote to Truman that, "as heads of the Governments which have control of this great force, we should without delay make a joint declaration of our intentions to utilize the existence of this great power. . . in the interests of all peoples in order to promote peace and justice in the world."[67]

Truman's reply was noncommittal and certainly stopped short of any acknowledgement that Britain should participate in the "control of this great force." After a similar exchange of correspondence in September/October, Attlee flew to Washington early in November to discuss the question in person with Truman. Mackenzie King, the Prime Minister of Canada, also joined the talks, which ended with a public call for the establishment of a United Nations Commission to make specific proposals for controlling atomic energy by limiting its use to peaceful purposes and eliminating atomic weapons from national armaments. Other agreements reached by the leaders were summarized in an unpublished memorandum, which, at least according to British interpretation, provided for full and effective cooperation between the three countries. The organs of cooperation set up during the war, the Combined Policy Committee (CPC) and the Combined Development Trust, were to continue functioning. The CPC was charged with the responsibility for recommending appropriate arrangements for the future.

Attlee and Anderson, his chief advisor on atomic questions, returned from Washington in an optimistic frame of mind; their optimism was, however, short-lived. The CPC met as planned but made very little progress toward the British goal of full cooperation. It soon became evident that the American policymakers had no intention of sharing the secrets of atomic design and construction with their British counterparts. The Americans were probably sincere in wishing to explore possibilities of placing atomic weaponry under responsible international control and may well have believed that to have divulged secrets to Britain would have undermined their efforts towards that objective. They were wary of those secrets in the hands of a socialist British government with its relations with, at that time, a predominantly socialist Europe. Moreover, they had to take note of the wishes of American politicians, who during the early months of 1946--and particularly after the revelations about the Canadian spy ring and the treachery of the British scientist Nunn May had broken in February--seemed gripped by a hysterical need to protect the secrecy of the U.S. atomic programme. The McMahon Act, the expression of this need, became increasingly restrictive as it passed through the House and Senate on its way to enactment in the summer of that year. Truman made no apparent effort to persuade the politicians to exempt Britain from the restrictions of the act and indeed claimed to Attlee that it had never been his intention to transmit details of the construction and operation of atomic plants to Britain and that Attlee had misinterpreted the agreements expressed in the November 1945 memorandum.[68] At a time when the demands on Britain's economy were becoming increasingly difficult to meet, the British policymakers, therefore, had to decide whether to leave the United States as the sole atomic power or whether to proceed independently to develop, test, and manufacture an atomic bomb with all of the capital and opportunity costs that that involved.

The decision to proceed with bomb production once American help could no longer be counted on was not taken lightly. It was true that by mid-1946, the groundwork had been laid for a national atomic energy programme: the Atomic Energy Research Establishment (AERE) had been set up as early as October 1945; in the first few months of 1946 an Atomic Energy Production Division had been set up in Risley, Lancashire, and a uranium processing plant at Springfield in the same county; and in the same year work had begun on the AERE site at Harwell, Berkshire, and an Atomic Energy Bill giving the Minister of Supply the powers to use and produce atomic energy had been passed through Parliament. However, whereas research and development in the uses of atomic energy could have been spread out over several years and undertaken with minimum effects on the rest of the economy, the rapid development of atomic bombs promised to be costly in terms of both money and resources. It was evident at the time that such a programme would require more than the £30 million estimated as the cost for a British programme in spring 1946 when there were still some hopes of a deal with America, and that it would have disruptive effects on the country's economic life by its demands on building labour, the engineering industry, and electricity.[69]

The formal decision to proceed with atomic bomb production and to give those responsible priority for the allocation of materials, metals, and labour was taken in January 1947, at the beginning of the year when Britain's postwar economic prospects were to appear bleakest of all. The decision taken was, therefore, one of importance. It did not represent merely an agreement to continue with an established program but was a conscious decision to use significant resources to give effect to a particular military objective. In reaching their decision not to stand back and allow the United States to remain the sole atomic power, the policymakers were obviously motivated by the fear that in any future European conflict, Britain might once again have to stand and fight alone, wondering if and when the United States would decide to intervene. This fear was reinforced not only by the fact of continuing U.S. troop withdrawals from Europe but also by memories of isolationist speeches given by U.S. politicians during debates on subjects such as the McMahon bill and on the loan to Britain. Perhaps the worst scenario the policymakers envisaged and wished to avoid was the possibility that Russia or some other potential adversary would develop an atomic bomb and would then threaten Britain, which would not have a watertight commitment from the United States to intervene on her behalf. On the other side of the coin, it was felt that British possession of an atomic bomb would be sufficient to deter either Russian or renewed German adventurism; simply to use the threat that Britain would call on the United States, that capricious "boy giant," to use its bomb against them was not considered at all as a reliable or effective deterrent.

The policymakers were also motivated by the feeling that since the atomic bomb was as much a British as it was an American invention, it would be unjust for the Americans alone to profit from it. In this context, proceeding with bomb production became a means of ensuring that Britain benefited from and did not waste resources it had already spent.

In most of the discussions that preceded the final decision to go ahead, an important additional argument was advanced, namely, that the atomic bomb had become the ultimate international status symbol and that possession of a bomb was absolutely essential if Britain was to retain her prestige and her reputation as one of the preeminent world powers in a totally different league from countries such as France. William Penney, the government scientist named to be in charge of the development of the British atomic bomb, clearly saw the justification for his job in the fact that "the discriminative test for a first-class power is whether it has made an atomic bomb and we have either got to pass the test or suffer a serious loss in prestige both inside this country and internationally."[70]

There were a few who argued against the development of an independent British bomb. Notable among them was Professor Blackett, a leading member of the Advisory Committee on Atomic Energy, who argued that given her weakened position in the postwar world, Britain would have to depend on American aid in any foreseeable major war and that the channelling of scarce resources into duplicating American bomb production made sense neither strategically nor economically.[71] Apparently Bevin dismissed Blackett with a contemptuous "he should stick to his science,"[72] and there is no evidence that his arguments were ever subjected to detailed analysis. Perhaps Blackett's problem was that, although he pointed to loopholes in the strictly military and economic arguments in favour of British atomic bomb production, he did not address himself to the question of the bomb as a symbol of first-class status in international relations--a major preoccupation of the policymakers.

The papers of the Cabinet Committee dealing with atomic research questions reveal that Ministers were concerned that it might prove difficult to divert necessary resources to atomic bomb production but were even more concerned that if production did not go ahead, British prestige in the world would decline. The possession or control of atomic weapons had become the sine qua non of great power status and real independence in the postwar world. Attlee in his memoirs first justified the decision to build a British atomic bomb by referring to the need "to hold up our position vis-à-vis the Americans."[73] Bevin at the time said that he couldn't "care a damn" about the strategic and economic arguments against proceeding with atomic bomb production, because "no other Foreign Secretary should have to sit in front of the U.S. Foreign Secretary and be talked to as I have been talked to by Byrnes. It shouldn't happen and the only way to stop it is to have plants in this country with the Union Jack on top."[74]

In spite of differences in a number of areas, most historians of this period seem to be agreed that the British decision to proceed with independent atomic bomb production was influenced not only by strictly strategic considerations but also by the perceived need to preserve Britain's prestige and appearance of world power. For example, Professor Gowing, who as the official historian of the programme has had the largest access to the official documents, concluded:

> When the British project was begun it was realized that it would cost a great deal. . . it was taken as axiomatic that the country must have a project, and the question whether it could be afforded did not arise. . . To Britain, possession of her own atomic deterrent was necessary to her first-class power status for political as well as military reasons.[75]

Groom in his analysis of British thinking about nuclear weapons observed that "atomic weapons seemed to be a symbol of first-class status to the British policymakers at the time. It therefore became a matter of national pride and prestige that Britain should acquire them."[76] Goldberg, an American writer, who interviewed many of those responsible for taking the decisions, concluded that "Failure to accept the challenge of atomic energy would have been interpreted as a retreat from greatness, an abandonment of power. The loss of prestige, influence, and international respect, it seemed to the leaders, would be greater than the nation could endure."[77]

From a strategic point of view, even with the benefit of hindsight, the British refusal to accept that the atomic bomb should remain the possession of the United States alone and, by 1949, of the United States and Russia, may or may not have been wise. Credible arguments exist for both points of view. If one accepts the argument that with the uncertainty about the degree of U.S. involvement in international affairs in the postwar world and with Russian designs on Western Europe similarly uncertain, possession of the atomic bomb could not be left uniquely with the United States; the question needs to be answered whether it was necessary for Britain alone to bear the burden of developing and producing an alternative bomb. Could the costs have been shared by cooperation with other Western European or even commonwealth countries, as some historians have suggested?[78] Admittedly, prospects of cooperation at that time seemed quite bleak. None of the dominions, not even Canada, whose Prime Minister had participated with Attlee in the talks about the bomb with Truman in 1945, had shown any really active interest in developing atomic weapons and France not only had pro-Moscow elements in its government but had also placed its nuclear programme in the hands of Frederic Joliot-Curie, an open Communist. Moreover, any spread of knowledge concerning the atom bomb to other countries would have been fiercely resisted by the United States, whose goodwill Britain required to facilitate her own programme.

But perhaps the possibility of persuading one or more of the dominions to participate or of approaching the French if and when the Communists fell out of the government could at least have been examined. In the available records there is no evidence of any discussions about such possibilities. One reason for that might well be that the British authorities wanted the bomb to be made in Britain alone so that it could serve as indisputable proof of the country's first-class world status. Although this objective might not have been crucial in weighing the scales towards a positive decision, it does seem to have had the effect of weakening any desire not only to share development costs with a country other than the United States but also to evaluate in depth the arguments against proceeding that Blackett and others had advanced.

THE MIDDLE EAST

Of all the areas requiring the elaboration of a policy stance in the immediate aftermath of the Second World War, one of the most important for the British authorities concerned the role to be played in the Middle East, where in 1945 Britain had troops and bases in most of the countries around the Eastern end of the Mediterranean, from Greece right around to Libya, and similarly, in many of the countries bordering the Red Sea, the Gulf of Aden and the Persian Gulf. During the period under review, significant decisions had to be taken with regard to several countries in that area: in 1945 and 1946 Britain took it upon herself to safeguard the independence of Syria and of Lebanon and to ensure that France did not return to reassert the League Mandate powers she had exercised between 1920 and the early days of the war; it fell upon Britain also to play a key role in resisting Russian designs on Iran; Egypt's desire to remove the last vestiges of British power and to assume control of the Sudan involved the policymakers in long negotiations throughout the period; and the problems of reconciling Jewish and Arab claims in Palestine proved to be even more complex and time-consuming. In fact, in one way or another, British policymakers were actively involved in most of the Middle Eastern states.

At the end of the war, as they considered Britain's future role in the Middle East as a whole, the policymakers received conflicting advice. On the one hand they were urged to consolidate British strength in the area on the grounds that any weakening would put not only oil supplies but also the integrity of the commonwealth at risk; on the other hand they were advised that the Mediterranean had lost its strategic importance and that troop withdrawals from the area were necessary if Britain's available economic and military resources were to be used most effectively. One of the most influential supporters of British withdrawal was the military strategist, Liddell Hart, who concluded that if Britain were to maintain its present strategic position in the Middle East it would need to provide forces several times greater than had been stationed there before the war. Since that was not possible and since the establishment of a combined force from several countries might tend to increase rather than decrease tensions in the area, he argued that a more hopeful course might be to negotiate with Russia for the Middle East to be declared a neutral zone. British troops could then consolidate in West Africa, poised to return to any part of the Middle East that came under threat.[79]

The debate about whether Britain should make a significant if not complete withdrawal from the Middle East began as the war ended and became quite lively by early 1946, but was subsequently relegated to the background as those taking a position against withdrawal proved immovable and as concern about Russian expansionism increased.[80] It could well be argued that the attitudes of the policymakers with regard to Britain's world role had some influence on the outcome of this debate, and that if those attitudes had been different in the early postwar years, not only could overseas expenditures have been cut considerably but also the later embarrassment of the Suez intervention might have been avoided.

The case for a significant withdrawal from the Mediterranean area was first taken up in the Cabinet by Dalton. Convinced that the prevailing level of expenditures in the Middle East was imposing increasing constraints on his domestic policy, he quickly saw withdrawal from the area as a desirable objective. In one typical diary entry he complained of the demands made for further resources to continue Britain's role in the Middle East and then exclaimed, "we are totally overstretched at present and just can't keep it up."[81] Dalton applauded any cutback in that area; for example, when the decision to withdraw from Palestine was taken he wrote, "This, if we stick to it, is a historic decision. We are drawing in our horns in the East Mediterranean."[82] Incidentally, in this same entry he castigated Bevin for his slowness in accepting withdrawal, and concluded that Bevin "has no credit out of this."

Next to Dalton the Minister involved in the foreign policy decisionmaking process with the keenest perception of the constraints imposed by overseas expenditure was the Prime Minister himself. Dalton obviously managed, on occasion, to convince Attlee of the strength of his case. In a diary entry in February 1946, he recorded:

> CRA is inclined to think that it is no good pretending any more that we can keep open the Mediterranean route in time of war. If this is so, it means we could pull troops out from Egypt, and the rest of the Middle East, as well as Greece. Nor

could we hope to defend Turkey, Iraq, or Persia against a
steady pressure of the Russian land masses. And if India "goes
her own way" before long, as she must, there will be still less
point in thinking of lines of Imperial communications through
the Suez Canal.[83]

Attlee tried to win support for some withdrawal from the Middle East
among his colleagues involved in defence and foreign policy questions and with
the military leaders. Bevin, according to Dalton, was at first interested in the
possibilities of withdrawing British troops from the Mediterranean area and
basing some of them in Kenya and Southern Africa where they could be ready
to return Northwards should the need arise. He was, however, soon won over
to the point of view of the military leaders and of most of his officials who were
strongly opposed to such a notion. In fact, Dalton and Attlee could find few real
allies; apart from isolated individuals such as Liddell Hart, the only other support
came from Treasury officials and from left-wing intellectuals and politicians,
neither of which group commanded total respect from those responsible for
foreign policy.

Bevin's failure to accept the case for withdrawal was predictable; he had
come to the Foreign Office predisposed to maintain a strong British presence in
the Middle East. Well before the end of the war, he made clear his view that the
area would be "the most dangerous part of the world in the next 50 years"
because it would be the meeting point of the "three great imperialisms."[84] Soon
after taking office, Bevin in a joint memorandum with George Hall, the Colonial
Secretary, wrote "The maintenance of our position in the Middle East remains
a cardinal feature of British policy and, in consequence, we must be prepared to
undertake the commitments and expenditure inherent in maintaining that
position."[85] Bevin, in fact, came to office determined to bring about change
and progress in the Middle Eastern area. One of the first memoranda sent to his
new staff was on the theme of "peasants not pashas" and called for British
influence to be used to improve general living standards in the area.[86] Bevin
quoted the need for a strong British position in the Middle East as a justification
for strong policies in Greece and India. For example, in one Cabinet paper
issued during a difficult phase of the Greek Civil War, he wrote that the most
overpowering reason for holding firm in Greece "is that we must maintain our
position in Greece as a part of our Middle East policy, and unless it is asserted
and settled it may have a bad effect on the whole of our Middle East
position."[87] Bevin used a similar justification for maintaining a strong position
in India at the Cabinet meeting of 5 June 1946.[88]

Bevin's preference for retaining a British presence in the Middle East
was reinforced by his officials at the Foreign Office, who, with some
justification, have often been accused of having romantic, pro-Arab
predispositions.[89] A Foreign Office briefing for the Chief of General Staff,

written before his tour of the Middle East in autumn 1945, demonstrates a
predilection for strengthening the British presence in the area rather than
reducing it:

> The fundamental principle which we want to bring home both
> to the Egyptians and to the Iraqis is that the defence of their
> country can only be assured by Anglo-Egyptian or Anglo-
> Iraqui partnership and that it is contrary to the interests of
> these countries themselves to insist on the exclusion of British
> forces from their territories in time of peace.

Britain, the briefing continued,

> is the only great power whose interests coincide with theirs and
> who, as an ally, would be willing to come to their aid. It may
> be that at some future date the UNO will be able to provide
> effectively for the defence of small countries, but that time has
> not yet arrived. Even when it does come, any operational
> forces of the UNO, if they are to be effective, would require
> precisely similar facilities.[90]

The War Office in its briefing for the same mission took an even
stronger line: "Britain as the great power most concerned in the maintenance of
peace and security of the region must continue to play the leading part in defence
arrangements in the Middle East." And then in a passage that showed a certain
unawareness of Britain's economic position, the briefing continued:

> The range of scientific research and the rate of development
> and production which was attained in the recent war is likely
> to be exceeded in any future war. It is evident therefore that
> only the great powers can hope to keep abreast with the
> modern methods of waging war. The forms of equipment now
> used. . . need a vast industry behind the fighting forces and
> development can only be achieved by having great industrial
> resources available. The expense involved is prodigious and
> therefore great financial resources too are required. All these
> can only be provided by a great power.[91]

Just as the War Office took a stronger line than did the Foreign Office
on this issue, so the arguments for remaining in the Middle East were expressed
even more strongly by Alexander, who, next to Attlee, was the senior Cabinet
spokesman on defence matters in the early postwar years. In January 1947 he
outlined what he saw as the three major objectives of British defence policy:

"The defence and safety of the United Kingdom, the maintenance of our sea communications and a firm hold on the Middle East area."[92] A few months later it was obvious that he had remained impervious to the representations that Dalton and Attlee had made to him. The Middle East, he said,

> remains a vital link in the communications and hence in the security of all parts of the British Commonwealth and our legitimate defence requirements must and will be safeguarded in that area. . . thus we find ourselves on the morrow of victory inextricably involved in commitments all over the world from which we can not separate ourselves if, as we must, we mean to take our full part in preserving order and rebuilding a world shattered by six years of total war.[93]

Some years later when Attlee attempted to analyze why his proposals for withdrawal from the Middle East had not been more successful, he placed the blame not on his Cabinet colleagues and the Foreign Office but quite squarely on the shoulders of the military leaders:

> Most of the military were inclined to put too much weight on the Middle East as a base. They overlooked the political issues and the facts of Arab nationalism and insisted that we must hang on to it as a vital main support area. Monty. . . still had a hangover from the days when the Middle East was the essential link between Britain and India. But India had ceased to be a British imperial place of arms and the Suez Canal had never been a particularly good waterway in war time. Monty overemphasized the importance of the Middle East from the strategic point of view.[94]

The strength of the military point of view was also recalled by Barclay: "Generally speaking Mr. Bevin accepted the views of our defence chiefs on the need to maintain our military presence in the area."[95] Cunningham, who, incidentally, had a house in Malta and a deep romantic attachment to the Mediterranean, made evident in his diary the strong feelings of the military leaders. Attlee's attempts to bring them to consider the possibilities of withdrawal from the Middle East was met with shock and incredulity. After a Defence Committee meeting at which Attlee had advanced his ideas, Cunningham recorded: "Attlee's attitude to the Mediterranean question is past belief. He doesn't seem to realize what the passage through the Mediterranean means to us. He seems to think it is an idea maintained for the benefit of the Navy."[96] The views of the Chiefs of Staff concerning the Middle East were well summarized in a joint memorandum they wrote concerning the revision of

the Anglo-Egyptian Treaty.   After explaining how Britain had twice saved
Europe because of its Middle Eastern presence, the three leaders concluded:

> We cannot get away from geography. It so happens that Egypt
> occupies a unique position in relation to the group of states
> known as the British Commonwealth of Nations. In the long
> run, therefore, the security of this area is as vital to the British
> as it is to the Egyptians themselves, and we surely cannot be
> expected to forego our minimum security requirements there.
> When one thinks of the steps that Russia has taken in the
> Baltic and the Balkan states to secure her frontiers, surely what
> we are asking in Egypt is a very little thing?
> s/ Alanbrooke
> Cunningham of Hyndhope
> Tedder[97]

The effect of attitudes is reflected in the fact that although the
arguments in favour of withdrawal were coherent and logical, they excited very
little deep evaluation amongst the groups opposed to withdrawal. Certainly there
was no thorough discussion of scaling down operations in the military and
strategic journals during the early postwar years. Philip Darby, after a detailed
study of the publications and writings of the time, concluded that "In general,
Parliament and press gave remarkably little thought to the possibility of limited
withdrawals and, with some notable exceptions, criticism of the Government's
defence policies focused on the adequacy of the effort rather than the breadth of
commitments." He quotes one official as admitting, "From 1945 to 1947 we
were preparing the Indians for the change but not ourselves."[98] He noted that
the Defence Committee made no serious attempt to reappraise the situation and
concluded that British leaders in general saw the new world as a continuation of
the old and that quite simply reappraisal was too fundamental to be practical
politics.

The arguments for withdrawal were clearly incompatible with a number
of the attitudes that have been described in earlier chapters. Withdrawal from
previously held positions did not square with the perceived need to enhance
Britain's role as a great world power; withdrawal would have devalued some of
the war's most popular victories, for example El Alamein and the other defeats
of Rommel; withdrawal would have invited the criticism that the many British
lives given to defend positions in the Middle East had been given in vain;
withdrawal for the convenience of the domestic economy could have been seen
as a return to the foreign policy of appeasement and retreat before foreign
pressures; in short, withdrawal from the Middle East would have represented an
admission of weakness and would not have contributed to the much sought after
illusion of strength.

The attitudes of those opposed to withdrawal were in harmony at the cognitive, affective, and action tendency levels, whereas the attitudes of those advocating withdrawal showed a certain amount of incongruity--more precisely, approval for withdrawal existed at a cognitive level but was not reinforced at an affective level. Attlee had cognitions that withdrawal would be in the interests of British economic recovery and that a continued presence in the Middle East was of less strategic value than it had been in the past; however, at an affective level, he was still very much attached to the concept of Britain playing the kind of role it had played during his youth. The fact that his cognitions were not reinforced at an affective level meant that he did not push his plans for withdrawal with any great force and did not stand up strongly against those who opposed him.

Because of the weakness of the attitudes supporting withdrawal, the attitudes opposing withdrawal were never subjected to detailed scrutiny. As a result, no positive decision to withdraw from the Mediterranean and Middle East area emerged from the debate. Admittedly, there was some talk in autumn 1946 of a shift in imperial strategy in the Middle East when the Foreign Office championed the idea that Britain could remove troops from those countries that would guarantee her the option of returning in the event of war.[99] This shift in strategy came about not as a result of a change in British attitudes but as a result of pressures from the Middle Eastern governments involved. It is true to say that the only withdrawals that were made came as a result of pressures from the governments of the countries in which British troops were stationed. Continued pretensions to a British role in the Middle East were, in the end, to do most to undermine the prestige that they were supposed to support.

Obviously, it has to be admitted that even if Bevin and his colleagues had accepted the need for a complete military withdrawal, the actual decisions they took in the early postwar period might not have been any different. It would probably have been decided, with good reason, that a rapid British withdrawal would have created a potentially dangerous vacuum. This fact was acknowledged by Liddell Hart, who, in explaining the reasons for his suggestions for a British withdrawal, wrote, "It seems to me that the essence of the issue in the Middle East lies in the question of flexibility-v-rigidity. The suggested reorientation is essentially a matter of a new conception to guide our steps."[100] Because of their attitudes, the policymakers were unwilling to embrace such a reorientation. It is because of that unwillingness rather than of their failure to take immediate action that the policymakers can be faulted. If only the need for a substantial withdrawal at the earliest feasible opportunity had been accepted, such a "new conception" would have made possible an earlier cutback in overseas expenditure and would also "have guided the steps" of the policymakers away from the path that was to lead inexorably to the humiliation of Suez.

WESTERN EUROPE

Finally, evidence of how the policymakers' view of Britain's world role influenced policy decisions can be seen in discussions concerning the country's relationship with Western Europe. The policymakers of the early postwar period have frequently been criticized for having failed to adapt themselves to the possibilities of political and economic union with the countries of Western Europe. If Britain could have taken advantage of the widespread support in Europe for the setting up of some kind of European supranational institution, it has been argued, she could have become a leading and founder member of any "Common Market," in which case she would have gone forward to enjoy an "economic miracle" of German magnitude and would thus have avoided the relative economic decline and crises that so characterized her postwar history. Although there are elements of truth in such arguments, too much must not be made of them.

The intellectual climate in continental Europe in the aftermath of the war certainly favoured the creation of a number of relatively small but highly articulate pressure groups united in their resolve to bring about some measure of federal organization in Europe. Some "federalists" were politically to the left, drawing their inspiration from the call by wartime resistance leaders for a "federal system for the European peoples."[101] Others were situated more on the centre and right of the political spectrum and were motivated by visions of peace and prosperity conjured up by Briand and Coudenhove-Kalergi during the interwar period and by the need they perceived to bring political unity to the states of Western Europe to prevent any further wars between them and to check further westward advance of the Soviet armies.[102]

Official support for federalist ideas was given by the governments of Belgium, Netherlands, and Luxembourg, but at least in the early postwar years, not by France or Italy and certainly not by the Scandinavian countries. Britain was not, therefore, alone at that time in wishing for a Europe united only by defensive treaties and "functional" agreements on matters of common interest that involved no surrender of sovereignty to a supranational authority. In fact, the British authorities made considerable efforts to bring about the closer unity of Europe. The Attlee Government at the close of its first term in office looked back with some justifiable pride at its achievements in that area. It had been the prime mover in bringing into being the Treaty of Dunkirk in 1947, which embodied mutual defence agreements between Britain and France; the Treaty of Brussels in 1948, which widened the treaty of the previous year to include the Benelux countries and which, in addition, called for increased social and cultural cooperation; and, most significant of all, the establishment of the North Atlantic Treaty Organization in 1949, which brought the United States and Canada into a framework for the defence of Western Europe. It could also look back to the positive role it had played in setting up the Organization for European Economic

Cooperation (OEEC) in 1948 to coordinate the European Recovery Programme and the distribution of Marshall Aid and perhaps with less justification to the formation of a Council of Europe, which provided a forum for discussion of topics of mutual interest to all European states.

In the early postwar years there were a number of justifiable reasons for rejecting British participation in any European federation. With regard to defence, there was no evidence that a federation would have provided a greater deterrent to the Russians than did firm defence treaties. Moreover, Britain was more vulnerable to attack by air than by any land campaign and it thus made more sense to try to keep a special relationship with the United States. As to economic matters, the standard of living was higher in Britain than in most other parts of Europe. In addition, with world demand far exceeding supply, membership in a European common market did not seem indispensable. A European federation, therefore, held no obvious economic attractions in the short term. Politically, the Labour Party had waited for many years for the chance to take over the reins of power and to put into effect its vision of a just society based on the principle of state planning and universally available social services. It would have seemed unnecessarily quixotic to have given up any portion of this power and freedom of manoeuvre to a supranational European institution.

Supporting a federal reorganization for Europe would have complicated still further the problems of the postwar settlement. How would Germany have been treated in any federation? What would have been the impact on the Russians whose goodwill in international affairs was still hoped for? How would the ongoing negotiations about Poland and the other satellite countries of Russia in Eastern Europe have been affected? In short, there were many sound reasons justifying a British rejection of ideas of political federation in the early postwar years.

The criticisms made of the policymakers' attitudes towards Europe in that period are not, however, completely unmerited because what debate there was on the validity of federalist ideas was concerned far more with subjective feelings than the hard facts of international affairs. Since, as Anthony Eden put it, the English felt "in their bones" that surrender of any sovereignty to a supranational European institution would be inappropriate, there seemed to be little point in analyzing the possibility in any great depth. If a thorough analysis had been made and the possible advantages of federation recognized, perhaps federation would not have been rejected in such an unqualified fashion, and the plans for establishing an economic community that were discussed in the mid-1950s--when many of the original reasons making it inappropriate for Britain to participate had declined in importance--might have been perceived more favorably. The attitudes of the policymakers with regard to Europe were not, therefore, insignificant in their effect upon Britain's subsequent economic and political history.

The debate about the possibilities of participating in a federally organized Western Europe was conducted at a much less serious level than the debate about British policies in the Middle East. There were some voices in the country favouring closer links with Europe, such as the academic Lionel Curtis and the Labour politician, R.W.G. Mackay, and there were some who took a directly opposing view and urged Britain to look to its empire and to steer away from entanglements in Europe, the source of so many of her past problems.[103] The vast majority of the population, however, including all those in positions of power, inasmuch as they thought about it at all took up positions in the middle ground.

The debate among the policymakers concerning relations with Europe focused on the degree of functional cooperation that would be desirable between Britain and her neighbours and the framework within which any alliances and agreements would be placed. The only Cabinet members showing any interest in supranationalism were Cripps and Bevan, who were both attracted to ideas of socialist internationalism and spoke on occasion of a "third force" that would have united the social democratic countries of Western Europe into a confederation--significantly, under British leadership--that would have been the equal of the United States or Russia. Neither Cripps or Bevan pushed these ideas with any force, however, and they were given scant attention by their colleagues. Attlee quickly dismissed their ideas as unrealistic. As he recalled to Francis Williams:

> Some of them thought we ought to concentrate all our efforts
> on building up a third force in Europe. Very nice no doubt,
> but there wasn't either a material or a spiritual basis for it at
> that time. What remained of Europe wasn't strong enough to
> stand up to Russia by itself. You had to have a world force
> because you were up against a world force.[104]

Bevin was firmly opposed to any federal organization of Europe, even though earlier in his life he had shown interest in such a concept.[105] As Foreign Secretary he saw it as his role to work for the strengthening of the British Commonwealth and to associate it with a Western European bloc of countries that would cooperate together as sovereign powers in reaching mutually acceptable objectives. Such an association, he believed, would enable Britain to maintain an influence in the world at least equal to that of the United States and Russia. He also envisaged building an alliance between this group of countries and the United States capable of defending the noncommunist world from Russian designs. The signing of the treaties of Dunkirk and Brussels and the creation of the OEEC and the North Atlantic Treaty Organization were the logical products of such ideas. Imbued with a grandiose vision of Britain's role in the world, it was quite logical that Bevin should be opposed to those advocating that Britain's long-term economic interests would best be served by its becoming a member of a European economic union organized on a supranational basis.

He was adamant that if Britain were to become a member of the planned Council of Europe, then the organization would have to be functional in nature with no supranational powers. His attitude to supranationalism was summed up in his well-known warning: "If you open that Pandora's box you never know what Trojan 'orses will jump out."[106] In his eyes the "federalists" were intellectuals and as such to be distrusted. He would not take Britain into "a talking shop"; Europe should be united through a process of evolution and not by the application of a constitution. The attitudes that predisposed Bevin against any serious consideration of British participation in a supranational European community were shared by his Cabinet colleagues. For example, Attlee favoured some kind of military alliance with the states of Western Europe, but only within a more general system of collective security.[107] He gave no real consideration to the possible advantages of rebuilding Europe on a federal basis as his earlier quoted reaction to the "Third Force" made clear. Attlee envisaged a Europe united more along the lines of the Congress of Vienna than of those laid down by Briand and the other federalists of the mid-twentieth century.

Bevin's senior political colleague at the Foreign Office, Hector McNeill, held proposals for European political integration in obvious disdain. Lord Gladwyn recalls that on hearing that he was considering taking up the post of Secretary General to the Council of Europe, McNeill asked indignantly

> whether I really thought that "Europe" was more important than the North Atlantic. . . It was my job, Hector suggested, to get on with that, and one day I might even have some hand in running it. Anyway, the idea of an "Atlantic Community" was the thing, and that of forming "Europe" was subsidiary. In 1948 this was a proposition which I did not really dispute, and indeed there were then few people in Whitehall who would have asserted the contrary.[108]

Gladwyn was certainly right in saying that few people in Whitehall would have asserted the contrary; in fact, few people in Whitehall asserted anything at all about the more radical ideas for the political and economic integration of Europe. Such ideas had very low salience at a time when there were still so many problems connected with postwar reconstruction on the home front and relations with America, Russia, and Germany abroad.

In an address to the Royal Institute for International Affairs in 1950, Christopher Mayhew, who had recently worked as Minister of State with Bevin in the Foreign Office, made clear the role attitudes played in the rejection of arguments in favour of European federalism:

When their [the West European states] regimes were "left," we
were urged on that account to merge with them to form a
Third Force bloc. We declined. Now that their regimes are of
the "right," we are urged to take what can only be regarded as
an irrevocable step towards federation with them. Again we
refuse. It is not ideology, but logic and commonsense, plus the
brute facts of Britain's world-wide entanglements. . . Our
approach to European unity has necessarily to be a functional,
empirical one--by intergovernmental agreement rather than by
federation, or by methods implying eventual federation.

Several years later, with the benefit of hindsight, Mayhew came to
believe that it was in fact his attitudes--his "logic and commonsense"--that made
the "brute facts of Britain's world-wide entanglements" a real obstacle to radical
innovations in British foreign policy. In 1967 he admitted:

It should have been obvious two decades ago--as soon as the
war ended--that a revolution in Britain's place in the world had
become inevitable. We should have seen then that in winning
a great military victory, we had suffered a great economic
defeat, and that the political influence we enjoyed owed more
to our past reputation than to any solid, continuing source of
international power. My own judgment was wrong at this
time. Like others, I looked to Britain to play a role in world
affairs which was in fact beyond her real powers.[109]

At the beginning of the 1970s Mayhew was prominent among those campaigning
for British entry into the European Community.
The possibility of British participation in a federally organized Europe
was never seriously considered by the Foreign Office in the early postwar years.
One reason was that with the pressure of work involved in deciding reactions to
events in the external environment, there was little capacity for thought on
longer-term or more philosophical problems. Moreover, no particular group of
officials was responsible for analyzing such issues. A question regarding
European unity sent to the Foreign Office for comment from the Prime
Minister's office was returned some weeks later with an apology: "The only
excuse is that this matter had to be dealt with by our United Nations Department,
who are at present completely overwhelmed by a flood of work."[110] Why it
could not have been dealt with by the department covering West European affairs
was not stated. Incidentally, Lord Strang's description of the state of mind of
Foreign Office officials at the time might help to explain the lack of
consideration given to such topics:

> Even in the sphere of foreign affairs, the mind revolted against the reading of discourses or articles that had no immediate bearing on day-to-day problems [also against]. . . aimless discussions at large about foreign affairs, whether inside the Office or outside. In all this the mind was attempting to shed all but the inescapable task of dealing with essential interviews or with the flow of papers and of reaching decisions on the matters of business carried by them and protecting its capacity to perform these functions come what might. . . I confess that when tired, I turned more willingly to administrative than to political problems.[111]

In view of this approach to his work, it is not surprising that according to the Foreign Office archives no serious analysis was made of the more innovative ideas about European unification. On taking office, Bevin instructed his officials to work towards establishing a "close association" with the countries of Western Europe, but uncertainties about Russian sensibilities and the strained nature of Anglo-French relations as a result of differences over the Ruhr and the Levant meant that little progress was made in this direction during 1945. The files for 1946 show that Foreign Office thinking had become set in the traditional mold. A number of defensive alliances of the pre-1914 style were to be created, and political and economic cooperation was to progress on a step-by-step basis, according to mutual need. No surrender of any part of national sovereignty was contemplated. Nigel Ronald summarized the current thinking; after explaining the advantages of fostering good relations between the nations of Western Europe in the fight to contain Russia, he wrote, "We must not blink the obvious fact that the real struggle is fundamentally an ideological one; social democracy versus communism." He then continued that the British authorities should decide clearly on their objective,

> that I think should be that the group should grow by accessions to an initial Anglo-French pact. The earliest accessories should be Belgium, Luxembourg, Netherlands, Norway, Denmark, and such parts of the British zone of Germany as we think is expedient to include, and ultimately Portugal and Spain when the latter has adopted a parliamentary democratic government.

A fellow Assistant Under-Secretary, G.F.A. Warner, in commenting on Ronald's minute, recommended that such ideas should be implemented in a gradual and non-dramatic manner: "We should. . . work quietly on specific projects of cooperation, thus giving the other powers a quiet 'lead'."[112]

When the question of European unification was addressed, the Foreign Office officials generally adopted the same functionalist approach as Bevin; for example, J. M. Troutbeck, commenting on some of the more innovative and far-reaching approaches to European organization, noted skeptically, "I believe the right method is to tackle particular difficulties rather than devise overall schemes. . . and particular difficulties *can* be smoothed out with patience, as the eventual conclusion of the satellite treaties has shown.[113]   The events of the ensuing years show that quite naturally it was this approach to Europe that prevailed. The treaties of Dunkirk and Brussels and the establishment of NATO were welcomed, but the Council of Europe was given only a grudging go-ahead and accepted only on the condition that it would be a consultative body with no authority over national governments.   The British authorities' rejection of supranationalism was demonstrated by their opposition to the European Coal and Steel Community and later, beyond Bevin's time, to the proposed European Defence Community and to the European Economic Community.

    In conclusion, although British reluctance to surrender any elements of its sovereignty to a European organization can be well understood in the circumstances of the late 1940s, it does seem apparent that the desire to keep an image of Britain as being on a distinctly superior plane to other European powers prevented the policymakers from evaluating seriously the possible advantages of British participation in some plans for European integration.   While this argument applies particularly to the policymakers of the 1950s, it applies also to those operating during the first few years after the war; if they had been able to accept more rapidly the economic consequences of the war and its likely effects on Britain's ability to assume the traditional world role to which they had become accustomed, they could have started the studies and discussions necessary to lay the groundwork for a future reorientation of British policy.   If a reorientation had been seriously considered in the 1940s, perhaps Britain could have had significant influence in the drafting of the Treaty of Rome in the 1950s and thus have avoided the humiliating rebuffs of the 1960s and, when finally joining the European Community in 1971, the need to accept rules that many perceived as being rather more favourable to the interests of the Community's original members than to those of Britain.

NOTES

1. PRO, FO/371/50807, U235/191/70, 31 December 1944.

2. See Owen (1945) p. 266, Underhill (1944) p. 295, Willcox (1943) pp. 24-27; and Fischer (1945) p. 100.

3. Crookshank Papers, Speech at Gainsborough, 3 July 1946.

4. Hobson (1902).

5. See the essay by Rita Hinden, Secretary of the Fabian Colonial Bureau 1940-1950, "Socialism and the Colonial World" in Creech-Jones (1959), pp. 9-18.

6. Creech-Jones (1959) pp. 23, 25-26.

7. Quoted in Louis (1977) p. 14.

8. Attlee Papers, Speech at Lord Mayor's Banquet, 10 November 1947.

9. Attlee (1961) pp. 53-54.

10. Attlee Papers, Speech at Lord Mayor's Banquet, 10 November 1947.

11. Quoted in Bullock (1960) p. 552.

12. MacDonald (1976) p. 113.

13. See, for example, Conservative Political Centre (1950) p. 144.

14. Cripps Papers, Election Broadcast, 20 June 1945.

15. Alexander Papers, Speech to Sea Cadets at Twickenham, 18 September 1947.

16. Donoughue and Jones (1973) p. 378.

17. Dalton Papers, Talk to the Fabian Society, November 1945.

18. Strachey, Speech at Diamond Jubilee of Fabian Society, 3 November 1946.

19. Shinwell (1955) p. 156.

20. Conservative Political Centre (1950) p. 41.

21. See *Commonwealth and Empire Review* 517 June 1946: p. 18, and Bartlett (1972) p. 11.

22. Bartlett (1972) p. 11.

23. Hankey Papers, File 2/6, 9 July 1947.

24. See Attlee Papers, Box 19, Speech at Lord Mayor's Luncheon, 9 November 1945 and Box 21, Speech to the Newspaper Society, 7 May 1946. See also MacDonald (1976) p. 119, and Huizinga (1958) p. 192.

25. Conservative Central Office (1950) p. 144.

26. Williams (1948) p. 184.

27. Goldsworthy (1971) p. 392.

28. Dalton Diary, 15 October 1948.

29. Franks (1955) p. 15.

30. Quoted in *United Empire* 38 (1947): p. 3.

31. R.I.I.A. (1946) p. 47.

32. Goldsworthy (1971) p. 392.

33. PRO, CP(46) 134, 30 March 1946.

34. Louis (1977) p. 15.

35. Mansergh (1958) p. 198.

36. Dulles and Riddinger, *Political Science Quarterly*, March 1955.

37. McCallum and Readman (1947) pp. 98-99.

38. PRO, CM(46), 55th Meeting, 5 June 1946.

39. Ibid.

40. PRO, CP(46) 222, 14 June 1946.

41. See, for example, CP(46) 229, 14 June 1946, and Attlee Papers, Box 7, Letter from Lord Salisbury, 25 December 1946.

42. PRO, FO/371/44559, AN/70/23/45.

43. PRO, FO/371/44606, AN/680/109/45, 12 March 1945.

44. PRO, FO/371/50809, U/1311/396/70.

45. Chuter-Ede Diary, 10 April 1945.

46. Donoughue and Jones, (1973) p. 253.

47. PRO, CP (46) 222.

48. Quoted in Williams (1961) pp. 118-119.

49. Dixon Diary, 25 July 1945.

50. Quoted in Williams (1961) p. 160.

51. See, for example, his speech in the House of Commons, 24 May 1946.

52. Alexander Papers, Diary for 16 April 1946.

53. PRO, Defence Committee Memoranda, DO (45) 4, 8 August 1945.

54. Francis Williams, for example, referred to it as "a carefully-timed act [that] must ... be seen as one of the most decisive strokes in the history of diplomacy," Williams (1952), p. 264. See also Shlaim, Jones, and Sainsbury (1977) p. 43.

55. Dalton Diary, 14 March 1947.

56. Petersen (1950) pp. 237, 253.

57. PRO, FO 371/45026, AS 1887/811/51, "British Policy in Latin America," Foreign Office Research Department Handbook.

58. PRO, FO/371/47450, N15473/10928/G.63, 10 November 1945, "British Policy towards Scandinavia."

59. Chalfont (1976) p. 288.

60. Cunningham Diary, 12 July 1945.

61. Attlee Papers, Speech to the United Nations Assembly, 10 October 1945.

62. Attlee Papers, Box 10, New Year message to "The Labour Woman," 31 December 1946.

63. Bevin Papers, Election Manifesto 1945.

64. PRO, CP (46) 222, 14 June 1946.

65. Gowing (1975) vol. 1, p. 164.

66. Ibid., p. 164.

67. Goldberg (1964) p. 410.

68. For a discussion of this issue, see Carlton (1976) pp. 164-172.

69. Expenditure on atomic energy between 1945 and 1953 amounted to some £159.3 million, about 11 percent of total Ministry of Supply expenditure and 0.44 percent of total expenditure on goods and services by Central Government and local authorities. See Gowing (1975), vol. 1, pp. 85, 87.

70. Gowing (1975) vol. 2, p. 500.

71. The memorandum in which Blackett first set out his views is quoted in full in Gowing (1975) vol. 2, pp. 194-206.

72. Quoted by M. Gowing in a speech at Leeds University reported in The Times, 11 October 1947.

73. Williams (1961) pp. 18-19.   See also "The Granada Historical Records" interview of 16 September 1965 published in 1967.

74. Howard (1978).

75. Gowing (1975) pp. 45, 499-500.

76. Groom (1975) p. 39.

77. Goldberg (1964) p. 427.

78. See Carlton (1976) p. 166. For useful background information on all aspects of atomic energy during this period, see also Pierre (1968).

79. Hankey Papers, "Africa or the Middle East? Reflections on Strategic and Peace Policy," Memorandum from B. H. Liddell Hart to Lord Hankey, 20 March 1946. See also Liddell Hart (1950) pp. 254-255.

80. See Monroe (1948) p. 129, and Mayhew (1950) p. 485.

81. Dalton Diary, 6 February 1947.

82. Dalton Diary, 20 September 1947.

83. Dalton Diary, 9 February 1946.

84. Quoted in Diamond (1974).

85. PRO, CAB 134/594, ORC (45) 21, 25 August 1945.

86. Williams (1961) p. 176.

87. PRO, CP (45) 107.

88. PRO, CM (46) 55, 5 June 1946.

89. See, for example, Connel (1958), p. 302.

90. PRO, WO 216/40, File 24/71.

91. PRO, WO 216/40, File 24/71.

92. Alexander Papers, Speech to RAC Dinner, 15 January 1947.

93. Alexander Papers, Speech to Overseas Empire Correspondents Association, 12 June 1947.

94. Williams (1961) p. 178.

95. Barclay (1975) p. 35.

96. Cunningham Diary, 16 February 1946.

97. CP (46) 224, 7 June 1946.

98. Darby (1973) pp. 19-20.

99. Sachar (1972) p. 407.

100. Hankey Papers, Letter from B. Liddell Hart, 2 July 1946.

101. Kitzinger (1967) pp. 29-33.

102. Aristide Briand (1862-1932) was a French statesman who served 11 times as Prime Minister of France. His work to encourage international cooperation and world peace brought him the Nobel Peace Prize in 1926. Toward the end of his life, he devoted much of his time to advocating a Federal Union of Europe. Count Coudenhove-Kalergi founded the Pan-European Union in 1923 and the European Parliamentary Union in 1947. He received the first Charlemagne Prize in 1950 and was named honorary Chairman of the European Movement in 1952.

103. See Mackay (London, 1948) and (Chicago, 1948). Some continental Europeans had at one time felt that a number of speeches given by Winston Churchill, particularly a radio speech of 1943 and an address in Zurich in 1946, gave evidence that Britain would be willing to join in a federal European organization. A closer look at Churchill's words, however, would have shown that in his view any supranationalism would cover the Continental countries only. "Britain," he said, "would not be a member of the 'United States of Europe', but together with America and hopefully with Russia would be its 'friend' and 'sponsor'." (See Kitzinger (1967) pp. 33-37.)

104. Attlee (1961) p. 171.

105. Bullock (1960) p. 55.

106. Barclay (1975) p. 67.

107. See "Foreign Policy and the Flying Bomb" PRO, CAB 66/53, WP (44) 414, 26 July 1944.

108. Gladwyn (1972) p. 206.

109. Mayhew (1967) pp. 11-12.

110. Attlee Papers, Box 5.

111. Strang (1955) p. 280.

112. PRO, FO/371 59911, Z2410/120/72, 13 March 1946.

113. PRO, FO/371, S9911, Z10754/120/72, 16 December 1946.

Part 5

Conclusion

11

Clinging to Grandeur

The purpose of this book has been to understand the origins and the influence of the attitudes of those responsible for taking foreign policy decisions in the early post-Second World War period. These attitudes that formed the frame of reference for the decision-making process can be summarized as follows:

- ▶ Britain's traditional role as a world great power should be maintained;
- ▶ Britain's influence in the world should not be less than that of America or Russia;
- ▶ Britain had evolved further in political and social terms than had other countries and was continuing to evolve;
- ▶ the determined foreign policies perceived to have been followed in the years preceding the First World War were worthy of emulation;
- ▶ the policies of the interwar period were characterized by weakness and vacillation and should not be emulated;
- ▶ any decision that could be interpreted as appeasement should be avoided or at least disguised;
- ▶ it was the interwar period and not the wars themselves that provided the major discontinuity in the flow of British history;
- ▶ the Battle of Britain and the "miracle" of Dunkirk marked Britain's arousal from lethargy and the first steps back to greatness;
- ▶ Britain showed her incomparable strength by standing alone against a powerful enemy;
- ▶ a country that had won the war could not possibly lose the peace;
- ▶ many of the values taught in Edwardian schooldays were appropriate and could be applied to decisions in the late 1940s;
- ▶ those who suffered or died during the war should not have done so in vain;
- ▶ Britain deserved the rewards of victory;
- ▶ Britain would always succeed in the end, no matter what the odds;

▸ a major aim of foreign policy should be to maintain British prestige;

▸ Britain was the "moral" leader of the world even if no longer the most powerful in military or economic terms;

▸ the empire and commonwealth should continue to be a source of strength and Britain should continue working for its development;

▸ the empire provided an excellent model for future world organizations;

▸ U.S. foreign policymakers were less skilled and less perceptive than their British counterparts;

▸ a combination of British brains and American muscle would prove ideal for the preservation of world peace;

▸ Russia wished to spread its political ideology and influence and should be resisted;

▸ Britain should never reduce overseas commitments if there was any danger of leaving a vacuum;

▸ Britain could not surrender sovereignty into the hands of a regional governing body; and

▸ foreign policy decisions should be taken on an empirical, pragmatic basis and not by applying specific ideological principles.

It has been argued in this study that different foreign policy decisions would in some cases probably have been taken if external events had remained the same but the policymakers' attitudes had been different. At the same time, it has been acknowledged that to determine the weight of attitudes in any decision taken requires a detailed multifactorial analysis. The message of the study is not that the policymakers made many wrong decisions in the aftermath of the Second World War. Indeed, if the policymakers could have been whisked into the future and then returned to their posts with the benefit of hindsight, they would probably have changed only a very few of the decisions they took. An excessively rapid rundown of overseas commitments could have been disastrous for the process of recreating international stability after years of chaos, and there were moral obligations to facilitate development in the poorer parts of the commonwealth, the abandonment of which would have required a totally uncharacteristic cynicism. In fact, the major criticism that can be applied to the policymakers of the early postwar years is not that they allowed their traditionalist attitudes to prevent them from making major adjustments to Britain's world role immediately but that they allowed them to delay recognition of the need for such adjustments in the foreseeable future.

This book demonstrates the value of psychological theory concerning attitudes in understanding how decisions were reached--or not reached--with regard to various foreign policy issues. By understanding the tensions created by cognitive dissonance and incongruity between cognitive and affective components of an attitude, it becomes easier to explain the vacillation, the postponement of decisions, the contradictory statements, the lack of motivation to study particular issues in depth, and other complexities that often make the dynamics of a decision-making process so difficult to understand.

This book has also demonstrated that in matters of foreign policy, the Labour Ministers were not "captured by their clerks." Both the leaders of the Labour Party with their self-image as the representatives of the working people of the country, and the Foreign Office mandarins, whose social origins were to a man either aristocratic or comfortably middle class, shared the same world view, the same *Weltanschauung*. Their ideas may have differed at a cognitive level in some areas, but at an affective level--the level at which attitudes had the most direct influence on action tendencies--they were very much united. They had all learned their history from the mouths of Whig teachers; they had all glanced proudly at the map in their classroom with so much of its area coloured pink; they had all felt a new surge of pride at British victories during the war. This identity of attitudes goes far to explain the broad consensus on foreign policy issues that Labour and Conservative governments have traditionally demonstrated. The degree of consensus between Cabinet and Civil Service was particularly high during the early postwar years; a fact that helps to explain the criticism of some contemporary back-bench Labour MPs that their leaders enjoyed associating with their civil servants and with political adversaries rather more than with members of their own party.

It is hoped that this book has made some contribution to the study of the effects of war on society. Marwick has developed an idea of Marx that war puts a nation to the test and that social systems that have outlived their vitality will collapse.[1] Because of its obvious failures, the National Socialist movement in Germany disintegrated almost completely in 1945. In Britain, things were very different. British institutions--the civil servants and a democratically elected government--were seen to have been responsible for a victory that became increasingly heroic as the months went by. The perceptions of Britain's war efforts undermined any predilections for radical reforms of the political system that the incoming socialist politicians might have nurtured in prewar days. What did not stand the test of war was the general approach to foreign policy that was seen to have characterized the twenties and thirties. The war in that sense provides a discontinuity, although in the intellectual climate of the times it was the interwar period that was the principal discontinuity in the flow of British history. The war was seen to have woken Britain from a period of lethargy and inaction. The strong motivation to fashion a foreign policy for the awakened Britain that would appear consistent with the one followed during the height of its world power proved an obstacle to acceptance of the fact that, in terms of its underlying economic position, the country was weaker at the end of the war than at the beginning. In short, war made an impact on the attitudes of the policymakers that probably influenced the type of decisions they took in the immediate postwar years.

Finally, in the years following the war, it appears that the main objective of the makers of British foreign policy was to maintain for the country as much power, prestige, and status as possible in world affairs. As a result, costly overseas commitments were only abandoned as a result of irresistible pressures from the external environment and never as a result of domestically initiated acts of policy. Possible radical changes in direction were never given serious attention, and for more than a decade after the war the search for international prestige and the defence of the status quo were continued with an ever-increasing cost to the country's real economic power. If the need for reorientation had been recognized sooner, Suez and some other inglorious British overseas entanglements in the 1950s and 1960s could have been avoided and the home economy would probably have flourished more without the burdens imposed by continuing high overseas expenditures. The relative decline of the British economy might also have been arrested or at least slowed down if the national temperament had been stimulated by the task of building a new world role rather than depressed by the failure to cling to the grandeur of the past.

NOTE

1. Marwick (1968 and 1974).

Part 6

Select Bibliography

ARCHIVES

Alexander, A. V., Papers, Churchill College, Cambridge.

Attlee, Clement R., Archives, Churchill College, Cambridge.

---, Papers, University College, Oxford.

Barrington-Ward, R., Papers, *The Times* Archives, London.

Bevin, Ernest, Papers, Churchill College, Cambridge.

Chuter-Ede, J., Diaries, British Museum, Additional Manuscripts 59690-59703.

Cunliffe-Lister, Philip, Papers, Churchill College, Cambridge.

Cunningham of Hyndhope, Diaries, British Museum, Additional Manuscripts 52557-52584.

Dalton, Hugh, Diaries and Papers, British Library of Political and Economic Science, London School of Economics.

Deakin, Ralph, Papers, *The Times* Archives, London.

Drax, Admiral Sir Reginald Plunkett Ernle-Erle, Papers, Churchill College, Cambridge.

Edwards, Admiral Sir Ralph, Papers, Churchill College, Cambridge.

Godfrey, Admiral J. H., Papers, Churchill College, Cambridge.

Grigg, Sir P. J., Papers, Churchill College, Cambridge.

Hankey, Colonel M.P.A., Papers, Churchill College, Cambridge.

Imperial War Museum collection of personal letters, diaries and memoirs: H. A. Baker Memoirs; Marjorie Barber Memoirs; S. L. Burstow Diaries; Margaret Crompton Journal of the War Years; E. C. Ealey Memoirs; A. F. Ebert Papers; Nina Evans Papers; M. V. Hazell Memoirs; W. E. Holl War Diary; Dr. J. P. McHutchison diaries; Mason Papers; June Meade Diaries; Kate Phipps war Diary; Strong Collection; Dr. C.J.G. Taylor Memoirs; and A.V.S. Yates Papers.

Liddell Hart, B. H., Papers, Kings College, London; also a limited number of papers at *The Times* Archive, London.

Hodsoll, Wing Commander Sir John, Papers, Churchill College, Cambridge.

Lyttleton, Oliver, Papers, Churchill College, Cambridge.

MacDonald, Iverach, Papers, *The Times* Archives, London.

Mallet, Sir Victor, Unpublished Memoir at Churchill College, Cambridge.

Maxwell Fyfe, Sir David, Papers, Churchill College, Cambridge.

Nuffield College Election Archive, Nuffield College, Oxford.

Parker, Ralph, Papers, *The Times* Archives, London.

Walter, J., Papers, *The Times* Archives, London.

SCHOOLBOOKS AND JUVENILE LITERATURE IN PRINT 1900-1914
(Place of publication London unless otherwise stated.)

Arnold's, *Arnold's Continuous Story Readers*, (1900).
---, *Arnold's Home and Abroad Readers*, (1904).
---, *Arnold's Junior Story Readers*, (1908-1914).
---, *The King Alfred Readers*, 8 volumes, (1900).
Baden-Powell, Sir R., *Scouting for Boys*, (1909).
Bell's, *Bell's History Readers*, 6 volumes, (1899-1914).
Berry, Albert J., *Britannia's Growth and Greatness*, (1913).
Blackie's, *Comprehensive History of England*, 4 volumes (1896).
---, *Story Book Readers*, (1905).
---, *Historical Readers*, (1883-1887).
Board of Education, "Suggestions for the Consideration of Teachers," in
     Parliamentary Papers, (1905) vol. 60.
Buxton, Etheldreda M. W., *Highroads of Empire History*, (1909).
---, *The Pageant of British History*, (1913).
---, *A Junior History of Great Britain*, (1910).
Chambers', *New Historical Readers*, (1891).
Finnemore, John, *Children of Empire*, (1905).
---, *The Empire's Children*, (1906).
---, *The Story of the English People*, (1905).
Kipling, R., and C.R.L. Fletcher, *A History of England*, (1911).
Le Feuve, Amy, *Us and our Empire*, (1911).
Nelson's, *Nelson's Supplementary Readers*, (1899).
Prothero, G. W., *Nelson's School History of Great Britain and Ireland*, (1908).
Temple, *Temple Infant Readers*, (1904).
---, *Temple History Readers*, 4 volumes, (1902-1904).
Tout, T. F., *Longman's Historical Series for Schools* (1902-).
Warner, George T., *A Short History of Great Britain*, (1906).
Yates, Matthew T., *Arnold's English Readers*, (1893).
---, *Arnold's History Readers*, (1894).
---, *Collins Alternative History Reader*, (1899).

SELECT BIBLIOGRAPHY OF OTHER WORKS CONSULTED
(Place of publication London unless otherwise stated.)

Abrams, Mark, "British Elite Attitudes and the European Common Market,"
     Public Opinion Quarterly 29, no. 2 (1965): 236-246.
Acheson, Dean, *Present at the Creation: My Years in the State Department*,
     (New York, 1969).

Acland, R., et al, *Keeping Left*, (1950).

Adamthwaite, Anthony, "Britain and the World 1945-1949: The View from the Foreign Office," *International Affairs* 61, no. 2: (1985).Amery, L. S., *The Washington Loan Agreement*, (1946).

Addison, Paul, *Now the War is Over: A Social History of Britain 1945-1951*, (1985).

---, *The Road to 1945*, (1975).

Adenauer, K., *Memoirs 1945-53*, (1966).

Adorno, Theodore W., *The Authoritarian Personality*, (New York, 1950).

Albrecht, Carrie Rene, "For an End to the 100 Years War," *Orbis* 14, no. 3 (1970): 627-641.

Allan, William, "G. A. Henty," *The Cornhill Magazine* 181, no. 1082 (1974): 71-100.

Allen, H. C., *The Anglo-American Predicament: The British Commonwealth, the USA and European Unity*, (1960).

---, *The Anglo-American Relationship Since 1783*, (1959).

Almond, Gabriel A., "The Resistance and Political Parties of Western Europe," *Political Science Quarterly* 63 (March 1947): 27-39.

---, and S. Verba, *The Civic Culture: Political Attitudes and Democracy in Five Nations*, (Boston 1965).

Ambrose, S. E., *Rise to Globalism*, (1971).

Amery, L. S., *The Awakening: Our Present Crisis and the Way Out*, (1948).

---, *My Political Life*, 3 volumes, (1955).

---, *The Washington Loan Agreement*, (1946).

Anderson, T. H., *The United States, Great Britain and the Cold War 1944-1947*, (1981).

Anstey, C., "The Projection of British Socialism: Foreign Office Publicity and American Opinion 1945-50," *Journal of Contemporary History* 19, no. 3 (1984): 417-451.

Ashton-Gwatkin, F.T.A., *The British Foreign Office*, (Syracuse, N.Y., 1949).

Aster, S., *1939: The Making of the Second World War*, (1973).

Attlee, Clement R., *As it Happened*, (1954).

---, "The Attitude of MPs and Active Peers," *Political Quarterly* (1959): 29-32.

---, *The Betrayal of Collective Security*, (1936).

---, "Civil Servants, Ministers, Parliament and the Public," in W. A. Robson, ed., *The Civil Service in Britain and France*, (1956).

---, *Clem Attlee: The Granada Historical Records Interviews*, (1967).

---, *Collective Security under the United Nations*, (1958).

---, *Economic History with Notes for Lecturers and Class Leaders*, (Published by ILP Information Committee circa 1925).

---, *Empire into Commonwealth*, (1961).

---, *I Want a Real Peace Conference to Deal with the Causes of War*, Labour Party Pamphlet, (1938).

---, *The Labour Party in Perspective*, (1937, revised 1949).

---, *Labour's Peace Aims*, (1939).

---, with Francis Williams, *A Prime Minister Remembers*, (1961).

---, *Twilight of Empire*, (New York, 1962).

Auld, J. W., "The Liberal Pro-Boers," *Journal of British Studies* 14, no. 2 (1975): 78-101.

Auriol, Vincent, *Journal du Septennat 1947-54*, (Paris, 1970).

---, *Mon Septennat 1947-54*, edited by Pierre Nora and Jacques Ozouf, (Paris, 1960)

Ayerst, David, *Guardian: Biography of a Newspaper*, (1971).

Bailey, Sidney D., ed., *British Party Organization*, (1952).

Baker, Ernest, *Age and Youth*, (1953).

Baker, George, *Mountbatten of Burma*, (1959).

Balfour, Michael, and John Mair, *Four Power Control in Germany and Austria 1945-1946*, (1956).

Ballam, H., and R. Lewis, *The Visitors' Book*, (1950).

Balogh, Thomas, "The International Economy" in *The British Economy 1945-1950* ed. by G.D.N. Worswick and P. H. Ady, (1952).

Barber, J. P., "British Foreign Policy: A Review of Some Recent Literature," *British Journal of International Studies* 1 (1975): 272-282.

---, and M. H. Smith, eds., *The Nature of Foreign Policy*, (1974).

Barclay, Roderick, *Ernest Bevin and the Foreign Office*, (Latimer, 1975).

Barker, Elizabeth, *Britain in a Divided Europe*, (1971).

---, *The British Between the Superpowers 1945-1950*, (1983).

Barker, Ernest, *The Character of England*, (1947).

---, *The Ideas and Ideals of the British Empire*, (1941).

---, *National Character*, (1928).

Barnes, H. E., *A History of Historical Writing*, (New York, 1962).

Barnett, Corelli, *The Audit of War*, (1986).

---, *The Collapse of British Power*, (1972).

Barnett, R. J., *The Alliance: America, Europe, Japan, Makers of the Postwar World*, (New York, 1983).

Barraclough, G., *History in a Changing World*, (Oxford, 1955).

Barratt-Brown, M., *After Imperialism*, (1963).

---, *The Economics of Imperialism*, (1974).

---, *Essays in Imperialism*, (1972).

Bartlett, C. J., *The Long Retreat: A Short History of British Defence Policy 1945-1970*, (1972).

Bayliss, J., *Anglo-American Defence Relations 1939-1980*, (1981).

---, "Britain and the Dunkirk Treaty: The Origins of Nato," *Journal of Strategic Studies* 5 (1982): 236-247.

Bell, P.M.H., "The Breakdown of the Alliance in 1940" in N. Waites, ed., *Troubled Neighbours*, (1971).

Beloff, Max, *An Intellectual in Politics*, (1970).

---, *New Dimensions in Foreign Policy*, (1961).

---, "The Role of the Higher Civil Service 1919-1939" in G. Peele and C. Cook, eds., *The Politics of Reappraisal*, (1975).

---, *The United States and the Unity of Europe*, (1963).

Beloff, N., *The General Says No*, (1963).

---, *Transit of Britain*, (1973).

Berners, Lord, *A Distant Prospect*, (1945).

Beveridge, Sir William, *The Price of Peace*, (1945).

Bevin, E., *The Britain I Want to See, Labour Party Pamphlet*, (1934).

---, *The War and the Workers*, (1940).

Bidault, G., *Resistance: The Political Autobiography of Georges Bidault*, (1967).

Binion, Rudolph, *Hitler Among the Germans*, (New York, 1976).

---, "Repeat Performance: A Psychohistorical Study of Leopold III and Belgian Neutrality," *History and Theory* 8 (1969): 213-259.

Birkenhead, Earl of, *Halifax*, (1965).

Birley, R., "The Undergrowth of History: Some Traditional Stories of English History Reconsidered," *Historical Association Pamphlet*, (1969).

Bjol, Erling, *La France Devant l'Europe: La Politique Europeenne de la Quatrieme Republique*, (Copenhagen, 1966).

Blackburn, Fred, *George Tomlinson*, (1954).

Blake, Robert, *The Decline of Power 1915-1964*, (1985).

Blum, John Morton, *From the Morgenthau Diaries: Years of War 1941-45*, (Boston, 1967).

Boardman, Robert and A.J.R. Groom (eds.), *The Management of Britain's External Relations*, (1973)

Bonnefous, Edouard, *L'Idee Europeenne et sa Realisation*, (Paris, 1950).

Booker, Christopher, *The Neophiliacs*, (1970).

Boothby, R., "The Loan Agreement," *National Review* 126 (1946): 118-125.

Borden, Mary, *Journey Down a Blind Alley*, (1948).

Boyle, P. G., "The British Foreign Office View of Soviet-American Relations 1945-1946," *Diplomatic History* 3 (1979): 307-320.

Bracken, Brendan, "Britain's Industrial and Economic Future," *United Empire* 36 (1945): 69-72.

Briggs, Asa, *The BBC, the First Fifty Years*, (Oxford, 1985).

Brittain, Sir Harry, *Pilgrims and Pioneers*, (1946).

Brockway, Fenner, *Outside the Right*, (1963).

Brogan, Colin, *The Democrat at the Breakfast Table*, (1946).

Brogan, D. W., *The Free State*, (1945).

Brome V., *Aneurin Bevan: A Biography*, (1953).

Bryant, Arthur, *The National Character*, (1934).

---, *Triumph in the West 1943-1946*, (1965).

Buckley, R., *Occupation Diplomacy: Britain, the United States and Japan, 1945-1952*, (1982).

Bull, Hedley, "What is the Commonwealth," *World Politics* 11, no. 4 (1959): 577-587.

Bullit, William, *For the President: Personal and Secret*, (Boston, 1972).

Bulloch, J., *MI5*, (1963).

Bullock, Alan, "Ernest Bevin, Foreign Secretary," *The Listener* (14 October 1982): 10-13.

---, *The Life and Times of Ernest Bevin*, 3 volumes, (1960, 1967, 1983).

Burn, W. L., *The Age of Equipoise*, (1964).

Burridge, T. D., *British Labour and Hitler's War*, (1977).

---, *Clement Attlee*, (1985).

Butler, J.R.M., *Lord Lothian*, (New York, 1960).

Butler, R.A.B., *The Art of the Possible*, (1971).

Byrnes, James F., *Speaking Frankly*, (New York, 1947).

Cadogan, E., *Before the Deluge*, (1961).

Cairncross, A. K., and B. Eichengreen, *Sterling in Decline*, (Oxford, 1983).

Calder, Angus, *The People's War*, (1969).

Calder, Jenni, *Chronicles of Conscience*, (1968).

Calvacoressi, Peter, *The British Experience 1945-1975*, (1978).

---, *Matters of Principle*, (1968).

Cammaerts, Emile, *Discoveries in England*, (1930).

Campbell, John, *Nye Bevan and the Mirage of British Socialism*, (1987).

Camps, Miriam, *Britain and the European Community 1955-1963*, (Princeton, N.J., 1964).

Cantril, Hadley, *Public Opinion 1939-1946*, (Princeton, N.J., 1951).

---, and W. Buchanan, *How Nations See Each Other*, (Urbana, Ill., 1953).

Capek, Karel, *Letters from England*, (1925).

Carlton, D., "Great Britain and Nuclear Weapons, the Academic Inquest," *British Journal of International Studies* 2, no. 2 (1976): 164-172.

Carr, E. H., *Nationalism and After*, (1945).

---, *The Soviet Impact on the Western World*, (1946).

---, *The Twenty Years Crisis*, (1939, revised edition 1946).

Carter, Gwendolen, *The British Commonwealth and World Security*, (Toronto, 1947).

CATO (Michael Foot, P. Howard, and F. Owen), *Guilty Men*, (1940).

Catroux, G., *J'ai Vu Tomber le Rideau de Fer*, (Paris 1952).

Chalfont, A., *Montgomery of Alamein*, (1976).

Chandos, Viscount, *The Memoirs of Lord Chandos*, (1962).

Charlton, M., *The Price of Victory*, (1983).

Cherry, Jack, *All the Cards on the Table*, (circa 1947).

Chester, D. N., and N. Bowring, *Questions in Parliament*, (Oxford, 1962).

---, and F.M.G. Wilson, *The Organization of British Central Government 1914-1956*, (1957).

Childs, David, *Britain Since 1945*, (1979).

Christiansen, Bjorn, *Attitudes Towards Foreign Affairs as a Function of Personality*, (Oslo, 1959).

Churchill, Winston S., *Europe Unite*, (1950).

---, *The Second World War*, 6 volumes, (1948 to 1954).

---, *Victory: War Speeches 1945*, (1946).

Citrine, Lord, *Two Careers*, (1967).

Clark, M. W., *Calculated Risk*, (1951).

Clark, William, *From Three Worlds*, (1986).

Clay, Lucius D., *Decision in Germany*, (Garden City, 1950).

Cohen, M. J., *Palestine and the Great Powers 1945-1948*, (Princeton, N.J., 1982).

Cohen-Portheim, P., *England, The Unknown Isle*, (1930).

Cole, G.D.H., *Europe and the Problem of Democracy*, (Peace Aims Pamphlet no. 44, 1947)

---, *The Intelligent Man's Guide to the Post-War World*, (1947).

---, *On Labour's Foreign Policy*, (1946).

Colton, J., *Leon Blum, Humanist in Politics*, (New York 1966).

Colville, J., *Footprints in Time*, (1976).

---, *The Fringes of Power: Downing Street Diaries 1939-1955*, (1985).

Connell, John, *The Office: A Study of British Foreign Policy and its Makers 1919-1951*, (1958).

Conservative Central Office, *Imperial Policy*, (1949).

Conservative Political Centre, *Conservatism 1945-1950*, (1950).

Cooke, Colin, *The Life of Richard Stafford Cripps*, (1957).

Cooper, Duff, *Old Men Forget*, (1953).

Coote, Colin, *Editorial*, (1965).

Cowling, M., *The Impact of Hitler*, (Cambridge, 1975).

Craig, G. A., and F. Gilbert, eds., *The Diplomats*, (Princeton, N.J., 1953).

Creech-Jones, Arthur, "A Labour View of British Colonial Policy," *United Empire* 36 (1945): 127-131.

---, ed., *New Fabian Colonial Essays*, (1959).

---, "Our African Territories," *United Empire*, 37 (1946): 110-113.

Crisp, Dorothy, *Why We Lost Singapore*, (1945).

Croft, Henry Page, *My Life of Strife*, (1949).

Cromwell, W. C., "The Marshall Plan, Britain and the Cold War," *Review of International Studies* 8 (1982): 233-250.

Crossman, R.H.S., "Britain and Western Europe," *Political Quarterly* 17 (January-March 1946): 1-12.

---, "The Lessons of 1945" in P. Anderson et al., *Towards Socialism*, (1965).

---, and Kenneth Younger, "Socialist Foreign Policy," *Fabian Tract* no. 287, (1951).

Cunningham, A. B., *The R.N.V.R. in War and Peace*, (1944).

---, *A Sailor's Odyssey*, (1951).

Curtis, Lionel, *World War: Its Cause and Cure*, (1945).

Cyr, Arthur, *British Foreign Policy and the Atlantic Area: The Techniques of Accomodation*, (New York, 1979).

Dahrendorf, Ralph, *Society and Democracy in Germany*, (1967).

Dallin, D. J., *The Big Three*, (1946).

Dalton, H., *Call Back Yesterday*, (1953).

---, *High Tide and After: Memoirs 1945-60*, (1962).

Darby, Phillip, *British Defence Policy East of Suez 1947-1968*, (1973).

Darwin, Bernard, *British Clubs*, (1943).

---, *The English Public School*, (1931).

Dawson, Raymond and Richard Rosecrance, "Theory and Reality in the Anglo-American Alliance," *World Politics* 19, no. 1 (1966).

Deacon, R., *A History of the British Secret Service*, (1969).

Deane, John R., *The Strange Alliance*, (New York, 1947).

Deane, P., and W. A. Cole, *British Economic Growth 1688-1959*, (1969).

De Gaulle, C., *Discours et Messages*, (Paris 1946).

---, *War Memoirs 1944-46*, (1960).

Delmas, Claude, "Le "Grand Tournant" de l'Histoire Britannique," *Revue de Defense Nationale* 27, no. 5 (1971): 728-739.

Deutsch, Karl W., and Richard L. Merritt, "Effects of Events on National and International Images," in Herbert C. Kelman, *International Behaviour: A Social-Psychological Analysis*, (New York, 1965).

Diamond, N., *The Foreign Policy of the Labour Party*, Unpublished M. Phil thesis, Leeds University, (1974).

Dibelius, W., *England*, (1930).

Dilks, David, ed., *The Diaries of Sir Alexander Cadogan*, (1971).

---, ed., *Retreat from Power: Studies in Britain's Foreign Policy of the Twentieth Century*, (1981).

Dixon, Piers, *Double Diploma: The Life of Sir Pierson Dixon*, (1968).

Dockrill, Michael, and John W. Young, *British Foreign Policy 1945-1956*, (New York, 1989).

Donoughue, B., and G. W. Jones, *Herbert Morrison*, (1973).

Dow, J., *Management of the British Economy 1945-1960*, (1964).

Doxat, John, *Shinwell Talking*, (1984).

Driberg T., *The Best of Both Worlds*, (1958).

Dulles, F. R., and G. E. Ridinger, "The Anti-Colonial Policies of Franklin D. Roosevelt," *Political Science Quarterly* 70, no. 1 (March 1955): 1-18.

Dulles, J. Foster, *War or Peace*, (New York, 1950).

Eastwood, G., *George Isaacs*, (n.d.).

Eayrs, James, *The Commonwealth and Suez: A Documentary Survey*, (1964).

---, *Fate and Will in Foreign Policy*, (1967).

Eden, Anthony, *The Eden Memoirs*, 3 volumes, (1960, 1962, 1965).

Ehrman, John, *Grand Strategy*, Volume 6, (1956).

Einzig, Paul, *Decline and Fall? Britain's Crisis in the Sixties*, (1969).

Eisenhower, D. D., *Crusade in Europe*, (1948).

Ellis, L. F., *Victory in the West*, 2 volumes, (1962, 1968).

Elton, Lord, *Imperial Commonwealth*, (1945).

Emerson, Rupert, *From Empire to Nation*, (1962).

Epstein, Leon D., *Britain, Uneasy Ally*, (Chicago, 1954).

Estorick, Eric, *Stafford Cripps*, (1949).

Evans, Trefor, *Bevin*, (1946).

---, ed., *The Killearn Diaries 1934-1946*, (1972).

Evens G. K., *Public Opinion on Colonial Affairs: A Survey Made in May and June 1948 for the Colonial Office*, (N.S. 119, U.K. Central Office of Information, June 1948, 1-16)

Ewer, E. N., "The Labour Government's Record on Foreign Policy," *Political Quarterly* 20 (April-June 1949): 117.

Farrel, J. C., and A. P. Smith, *Image and Reality in World Politics*, (New York, 1967).

Farrell, R. Barry, ed., *Approaches to Comparative and International Politics*, (Evanston, 1966).

Feis, Herbert, *Between War and Peace: The Potsdam Conference*, (Princeton, N.J., 1960).

---, *Churchill, Roosevelt and Stalin*, (Princeton, N.J., 1957).

Ferguson, John, ed., *War and the Creative Arts*, (1972).

Finer, S. E., H. Berrington, and D. Bartholomew, *Backbench Opinion in the House of Commons*, (Oxford, 1961).

Fischer, John, "Odds Against Another War," *Harpers Magazine* (August 1945): 100.

Fitzgerald, Walter, *The New Europe*, (1945).

Fitzsimmons, M. A., "British Labour in Search of a Socialist Foreign Policy," *Review of Politics* 12 (1950): 197-214.

---, *Empire by Treaty*, (1965).

---, *The Foreign Policy of the British Labour Government 1945-1951*, (Notre Dame, Ind., 1953).

Fleming, D. F., *The Cold War and its Origins 1917 to 1960*, 2 volumes, (1968).

Foot, Michael, *Aneurin Bevan*, 2 volumes, (1962).

Fox, A. B., and W.T.R. Fox, *Britain and America in the Era of Total Diplomacy*, (Princeton, N.J., 1952).

Fox, William T. R., *The Super Powers*, (New York, 1944).

Frankel, Joseph, *British Foreign Policy 1945-1973*, (1975).

---, *Contemporary International Theory and the Behaviour of States*, (1973).

---, "The Intellectual Framework of British Foreign Policy" in K. Kaiser and R. Morgan, eds., *Britain and West Germany*, (1971).

---, *International Politics: Conflict and Harmony*, (1969).

---, *The Making of Foreign Policy*, (1963).

Franks, Sir Oliver S., *Britain and the Tide of World Affairs: Reith Lectures 1954*, (1955).

Friedmann W., *The Allied Military Government of Germany*, (1947).

Gallacher, William, *The Last Memoirs of William Gallacher*, (1966).

Gallup, *Gallup Polls 1935-1971*, (New York, 1972).

Gamble, A., *The Conservative Nation*, (1974).

Gannon, F. R., *The British Press and Germany 1936-1939*, (Oxford, 1971).

Gardner, R. N., *Sterling Dollar Diplomacy: Anglo-American Collaboration in the Reconstruction of Multilateral Trade*, (Oxford, 1956).

George VI, *King George VI to his Peoples 1936-1951*, (1952).

Geyl, P., *Debates with Historians*, (1970).

Gibson, Guy, *Enemy Coast Ahead*, (1945).

Gilbert, M., ed., *A Century of Conflict 1850-1950*, (1966).

Ginsberg, Benjamin, *The Captive Public*, (New York, 1986).

Gladwyn, H.M.G. Jebb, *The European Idea*, (1966).

Gladwyn, Lord, *The Memoirs of Lord Gladwyn*, (1972).

Golant, W., "The Emergence of C.R. Attlee as Leader of the Parliamentary Labour Party in 1935," *Historical Journal* 13 (1970): 320.

Goldberg, Alfred, "The Atomic Origins of the British Nuclear Deterrent," *International Affairs* 40, no. 3 (July 1964): 409-429.

Goldstein, W., "British Defence and Alliance Strategy: The Strategic Quandary of a Middle Power," *Polity* 3, no. 2 (1970): 141-174.

---, *The Dilemma of British Defence: The Imbalance between Commitments and Resources*, (Columbus, 1966).

Goldsworthy, D., *Colonial Issues in British Politics*, (1971).

Gooch, John, "Attitudes to War in Late Victorian and Edwardian England" in Brian Bond and Ian Toy, eds., *War and Society, A Yearbook of Military History*, (1975).

Goodhart, Philip, *The 1922*, (1973).

Gordon, Michael, *Conflict and Consensus in Labour's Foreign Policy 1914-1965*, (Stanford, 1969).

Gore, Booth, Rt. Hon. Lord, "Obituary Notice of Sir Alexander Cadogan in *The Balliol College Record*, (1969).

Gowing, Margaret, *Independence and Deterrence: Britain and Atomic Energy*, 2 volumes, (1975).

Graebner, Walter, "Beaucoup Plus Vieux, Beaucoup Plus Sages," *France Libre* (May 1945): 40-44.

Granada Television, Granada Historical Records, *Interview with C. R. Attlee, 16 September 1965*, (1967).

Grant, Hugo, *Britain in Tomorrow's World*, (1969).

Granzow, Brigitte, *A Mirror of Naziism: British Opinion and the Emergence of Hitler 1929-1933*, (1964).

Gray, H. B., *The Public Schools and the Empire*, (1913).

Greenwood, David, "Constraints and Choices in the Transformation of Britain's Defence Effort Since 1945," *British Journal of International Studies* 2, no. 1 (1976).

Greenwood, S., "Ernest Bevin, France and Western Union August 1945-February 1946," *European History Quarterly* 14, no. 3 (1984).

Gregory, R. L., *Eye and Brain*, (New York, 1966).

Griffiths, James, *Pages from Memory*, (1969).

Grigg, Sir E., *British Foreign Policy*, (1944).

Groom, A.J.R., *British Thinking about Nuclear Weapons*, (1975).

---, *The Management of Britain's External Relations*, (1973).

Grosser, Alfred, *Western Germany from Defeat to Rearmament*, (1955).

Grundy, G. B., *Fifty-Five Years at Oxford*, (1945).

Gupta, Partha S., *Imperialism and the British Labour Movement 1914-1964*, (1975).

---, "Imperialism and the Labour Government" in J. Winter, ed., *The Working Class in Modern British History*, (Cambridge, 1983).

Guttsman, W. L., *The British Political Elite*, (1963).

---, *The English Ruling Class*, (1969).

Hall, J.E.D., *Labour's First Year*, (1947).

Hall, Noel F., "Colonial Development and Welfare: The Emergence of a New British Policy," *London Quarterly World Affairs* 12, no.2 (July 1946): 129-134.

Halloran, J. D., *Attitude Formation and Change*, (Leicester, 1967).

Hancock, Sir K., *Smuts*, 2 volumes, (Cambridge, 1962 and 1968).

Hannah, C. L., "Prejudice and the Teaching of History," in M. Ballard, ed., *New Movements in the Study and Teaching of History*, (1970).

Harlow, Vincent, *The British Colonial Empire and the British Public*, (1948).

---, *The British Colonies*, (Oxford Pamphlets on World Affairs, 1944).

Harrington, W., and P. Young, *The 1945 Revolution*, (1978).

Harris, K., *Attlee*, (1982).

Harris, N., *Beliefs in Society: The Problem of Ideology*, (1968).

Harrison, Tom, "British Opinion Moves Towards a New Synthesis," *Public Opinion Quarterly* 11, no.3 (Fall 1947): 327-341.

---, "The British Soldier: Changing Attitudes and Ideas," *British Journal of Psychology* 35, no. 2 (January 1945): 33-39.

Harrod, R. F., *The British Economy*, (1963).

---, *The Life of John Maynard Keynes*, (1951).

Hartley, Anthony, *A State of England*, (1963).

Harvey, G. E., *British Rule in Burma*, (1946).

Harvey, J. ed., *The Diplomatic Diaries of Oliver Harvey*, (1970).

Haseler, Stephen, *The Death of British Democracy*, (1976).

---, *The Gaitskellites*, (1966).

Hatch, Alden P., *The Mountbattens*, (1966).

Hathaway, R. M., *Ambiguous Partnership: Britain and America 1944-1947*, (New York, 1981).

Healey, Denis, "The Political Aspect," *Fabian Quarterly* (Summer 1948): 7-8.

---, et al., *Cards on the Table*, (A Labour Party Pamphlet, 1946).

Heiser, H. J., *British Policy with regard to the Unification Efforts on the European Continent*, (Leyden, 1959).

Henderson, James L., *A Bridge Across Time: The Role of Myths in History*, (1975).

Henderson, Sir Nicholas, "Britain's Decline: Its Causes and Consequences," *The Economist* 2 June 1979, 29-40.

Hertz, F., *Nationality in History and Politics*, (1944).

Hewison, R., *In Anger: Culture in the Cold War*, (1981).

Hibberd, Stuart, *This is London*, (1950).

Hirsch, Etienne, "L'Angleterre Fera-t-Elle Anti-Chambre?," *Les Cahiers de la Republique* 51 (January 1963): 9.

Hobson, J., *Imperialism*, (1902).

Hodson, J. L., *The Sea and the Land*, (1945).

Hoffman, J. D., *The Conservative Party in Opposition 1945-1951*, (1964).

Hoffman, Stanley, ed., *Contemporary Theory in International Relations*, (Englewood Cliffs, N.J., 1960).

---, "The Effects of World War Two on French Society and Politics," *French Historical Studies* 2, no. 1 (April 1961).

Hole, W. G., *John Englishman: An Appreciation*, (Cambridge University Press, 1946).

Hollis, L., *One Marine's Tale*, (1956).

Holmes, Jack E., *The Mood/Interest Theory of American Foreign Policy*, (Lexington, 1985).

Holsti, K. J., *International Politics: A Framework for Analysis*, (Chicago, 1972).

---, "National Role Conceptions in the Study of Foreign Policy," *International Studies Quarterly* 14, no. 3 (September 1970): 233-309.

Hopkins, H., *The New Look: A Social History of the 40s and 50s in Britain*, (1963).

Horne, Donald, *God is an Englishman*, (1970).

Horner, Arthur, *Incorrigible Rebel*, (1960).

Hough, R., *Mountbatten: Hero of our Times*, (1980).

Household, H. W., "The Patriot of the Future," *Parents Review* (June 1945): 147-150.

Howard, Michael, "Civil-Military Relations in Great Britain and the United States 1945-1958," *Political Science Quarterly* 75, no. 1 (March 1960): 35-46.

---, *The Continental Commitment*, (1972).

---, "The Quiet Archivist of the Air Force," *Sunday Times*, 19 March 1978, 39.

Howarth, T.E.B., *Prospect and Reality: Great Britain 1945-1955*, (1985).

Howell, D., *British Social Democracy*, (1976).

Hughes, Emrys, *Sidney Silverman, Rebel in Parliament*, (1969).

Huizinga, J. H., *Confessions of a European in England*, (1958).

Hull, C., *The Memoirs of Cordell Hull*, (1948).

Hunt, David, *On the Spot: An Ambassador Remembers*, (1975).

Hynes, Samuel, *The Edwardian Turn of Mind*, (1968).

Ireland, T. P., *Creating the Entangling Alliance: The Origins of the North Atlantic Treaty Organization*, (1981).

Iremonger, F. A., *William Temple*, (1948).

Irvine, Magnus, *The Britain of Tomorrow*, (1945).

Ismay, General the Lord, *The Memoirs of General the Lord Ismay*, (1960).

Jacob, Edward I. C., *The BBC a National and International Force*, (1957).

Janis, I. L., *Air War and Emotional Stress*, (New York, 1951).

Jellinek, Fred, "Foreigners' Britain," *National Review* (July 1945): 42-52.

Jenkins, Mark, *Bevanism: Labour's High Tide*, (1979).

Jenkins, Roy, *Afternoon on the Potomac*, (New Haven, Conn., 1972).

---, "British Foreign Policy Since 1945," *Proceedings of the British Academy* no. 58 (1972): 153-162.

---, "Ernest Bevin," *The Times*, 7 June 1971.

---, *In Pursuit of Progress*, (1953).

---, *Mr. Attlee*, (1948).

Johnson, F. A., *Defence by Committee*, (1960).

Joll, James, ed., *Britain and Europe*, (1950).

Joll, James, *1914, the Unspoken Assumptions*, (1967).

Jones, G. V., "The English as Others See Them," *Congregational Quarterly* (April 1945): 107-121.

Jones, P., *Britain and Palestine 1914-1948: Archival Sources for the History of the British Mandate*, (1979).

Jones, Roy E., *The Changing Structure of British Foreign Policy*, (1974).

Jones, Sir L. E., *An Edwardian Youth*, (1956).

Jones, Thomas, *A Diary with Letters 1931-50*, (1954).

Judd, D., *King George VI, 1895-1952*, (1982).

Juin, Alphonse, *Memoires*, (Paris, 1960).

Kahler, Miles, *Decolonization in Britain and France: The Domestic Consequences of International Relations*, (Princeton, N.J., 1984).

Kaiser, Karl, and R. Morgan, *Britain and West Germany: Changing Societies and the Future of Foreign Policy*, (1971).

Kantorowicz, Hermann, *The Spirit of British Policy*, (1931).

Kelly, Sir David, *The Hungry Sheep*, (1955).

---, *The Ruling Few or the Human Background to Diplomacy*, (1953).

Kelman, Herbert, ed., *International Behavior: A Social Psychological Analysis*, (New York, 1965).

Kennan, George, *Memoirs, 1925-50*, (Boston, 1967).

Kennedy, A. L., "Reorganization of the Foreign Service," *Quarterly Review* (October 1945): 397-412.

Kennedy, P. M., "The Decline of Nationalistic History in the West," *Journal of Contemporary History* 8, no. 1 (1973): 77-100.

---, *The Realities Behind Diplomacy: Background Influences on British External Policy 1865-1980*, (1981).

---, *The Rise and Fall of British Naval Mastery*, (1976).

---, "The Tradition of Appeasement in British Foreign Policy 1865-1939," *British Journal of International Studies* 2, no. 3 (October 1976): 195-215.

Keun, Odette, *I Discover the English*, (1934).

Kilmuir, Lord, *Political Adventure*, (1964).

Kimche, Jon, *Seven Fallen Pillars*, (1953).

King, Cecil H., *With Malice Toward None*, (1970).

King-Hall, S., "Russia's Place in the Post-War World," *Fortnightly* 164 (August 1945): 77.

King, F. P., *The New Internationalism, Allied Policy and the European Peace 1939-1954*, (1973).

Kirkpatrick, Sir Ivone, *The Inner Circle*, (1959).

Kitzinger, U., *Diplomacy and Persuasion: How Britain Joined the Common Market*, (1973).

---, *The European Common Market and Community*, (New York, 1967).

Knatchbull-Hugessen, Sir Hughe, *Diplomat in Peace and War*, (1949).

Koestler, Arthur, "Birth of a Myth," *Horizon* 8, no. 40 (1943): 227-243.

Kosoulas, D. George, *Revolution and Defeat: The Story of the Greek Communist Party*, (1965).

Labour Party, *Annual Conference Reports*, (annual).

---, *The Colonies*, (1943).

---, *Discussion Series no. 11: Approach to Foreign Policy*, (1946).

---, N.E.C., *European Unity: A Statement by the National Executive Committee of the British Labour Party*, (1950).

Langer, W. L., *The Diplomacy of Imperialism*, (New York, 1965).

Lapie, P. O., *De Leon Blum a De Gaulle*, (Paris, 1971).

Laski, Harold, *Will the Peace Last?*, (1944).

---, "Socialism as Internationalism," *Fabian Research Series* no. 132, (1949).

Lawson, C. P., "The British in India: Their Present, Their Future," *Asiatic Review* (October 1945): 359-368.

Leahy, W., *I was There*, (1950).

Lee, Jennie, *My Life with Nye*, (1980).

---, *This Great Journey: Autobiography 1904-1945*, (1963).

Lee, J. M., *Colonial Development and Good Government*, (Oxford, 1967).

Lehmann, John, *I am my Brother*, (1960).

Leifer, Michael, ed., *Constraints and Adjustments in British Foreign Policy*, (1972).

Leith-Ross, Sir F. W., *Money Talks*, (1968).

Lerner, D., *Euratlantica: Changing Perspectives of the European Elites*, (Cambridge, Mass., 1969).

Levering, Ralph B., *The Public and American Foreign Policy 1918-1978*, (New York, 1978).

Lewin, R., *The Chief: Field Marshal Lord Wavell, Commander in Chief and Viceroy 1939-1947*, (1980).

Liddell Hart, B. H., *Defence of the West*, (1950).

---, *The Memoirs*, 2 volumes, (1965).

Lieber, R. J., *British Politics and European Unity: Parties, Elites and Pressure Groups*, (Berkeley, Calif., 1970).

Lindsay, Sir II., ed., *British Commonwealth Objectives*, (1946).

Lipgens, W., *A History of European Integration: the Formation of the European Unity Movement 1945-1947*, (Oxford, 1982).

Louis, Roger, *The British Empire in the Middle East 1945-1951*, (Oxford, 1984).

Louis, W. R., *Imperialism at Bay: The United States and the Decolonization of the British Empire 1941-1945*, (1977).

Low, David, *Low Visibility: A Cartoon History 1945-1953*, (1953).

Lubbock, P., *Shades of Eton*, (1928).

Lyon, P., *Britain and Canada*, (1976).

McCallum, R. B., and Alison Readman, *The British General Election of 1945*, (1947).

McCurrach, D. F., "Britain's U.S. Dollar Problem 1939-45," *Economic Journal* 53 (1948): 356-368.

MacDonald, Iverach, *A Man of The Times*, (1976).

McEachran, F., "What the English Stand For," *Nineteenth Century* (June 1945): 253-257.

McFarland, S. L., "A Peripheral View of the Origins of the Cold War: The Crisis in Iran 1941-1947," *Diplomatic History* 4 (1980): 333-352.

McGovern, John, *Neither Fear nor Favour*, (1960).

McLachlan, D., *In the Chair: Barrington Ward of* The Times *1927-1948*, (1971).

---, *Room 39*, (1968).

MacLaren-Ross, Julian, *Memoirs of the '40s*, (1965).

McNeill, W. H., *America, Britain and Russia: Their Cooperation and Conflict 1941-1946*, (1953).

Mackay, R.W.G., *Britain in Wonderland*, (1948).

---, *You Can't Turn the Clock Back*, (Chicago, 1948).

Macmillan, Harold, *The Blast of War*, (1967).

---, *Tides of Fortune 1945-1955,*"(1969).

Madariaga, Salvador de, *Victors Beware*, (1946).

Maddison, Angus, *Economic Growth in the West*, (1964).

Maillaud, Pierre, *The English Way*, (1945).

Maisky, Ivan, *Memoirs of a Soviet Ambassador*, (1967).

Mallaby, Sir George, *From My Level*, (1965).

Mallalieu, William C., *British Reconstruction and American Policy 1945-1955*, (1956).

Mansergh, Nicholas, ed., *Documents and Speeches on British Commonwealth Affairs, 1931-1952*, (1953).

---, *Survey of British Commonwealth Affairs: Problems of Wartime Cooperation and Post-War Change 1939-1952*, (1958).

Margolis, Michael, and Gary A. Mauser, *Manipulating Public Opinion*, (Pacific Grove, Calif., 1989).

Marlowe, J., *Anglo-Egyptian Relations*, (1956).

---, *Britain in the Persian Gulf*, (1961).

Martin, David E., and D. Rubinstein, eds., *Ideology and the Labour Movement*, (1979).

Martin, Kingsley, *Editor: Autobiography 1931-1945*, (1968).

---, *Harold Laski*, (1953).

Martin, L. W., "British Defence Policy: The Long Recessional," *Adelphi Papers* no. 61 (November 1969).

Marwick, Arthur, *Britain in the Century of Total War*, (1968).

---, *British Society Since 1945*, (1982).

---, *The Explosion of British Society 1914-1962*, (1963).

---, *The Home Front: The British and the Second World War*, (1977).

---, "L'Impact de la Deuxieme Guerre Mondiale sur le Britanniques," *Revue d'Histoire de la Deuxieme Guerre Mondiale* 23, no. 90 (April 1973): 53-69.

---, "Middle Opinion in the Thirties," *English Historical Review* 89, no. 2 (April 1964): 285-298.

---, *The Nature of History*, (1970).

Mass Observation, *The Journey Home*, (1944).

---, "Portrait of an American," *International Journal of Opinion and Attitude Research* 1 (June 1947): 96.

---, *The Press and its Readers*, (1949).

Mathews, R.C.O., "Why Has Britain Had Full Employment Since the War?," *Economic Journal* 77, no. 3 (1968): 555-569.

May, E., *Lessons of the Past*, (1973).

Mayhew, Christopher, *Britain's Role Tomorrow*, (1967).

---, "British Foreign Policy since 1945," *International Affairs* 26 (October 1950): 447-486.

---, *Time to Explain*, (1987).

Medlicott, W. N., *British Foreign Policy Since Versailles 1919-1963*, (1968).

Meehan, Eugene J., *The British Left Wing and Foreign Policy*, (New Brunswick, Conn., 1960).

Mikado, I., et al., *Keep Left*, (1947).

Miliband, R., *Parliamentary Socialism*, (1962).

---, *The State in Capitalist Society*, (1968).

Millis, Walter ed., *The Forrestal Diaries*, (1952).

Milward, Alan, *The Economic Effects of the World Wars on Britain*, (1970).

Minney, R. J., *The Private Papers of Hore-Belisha*, (1960).

---, *Viscount Addison: Leader of the Lords*, (1958).

Molony, J. Chartres, "Evolution Without Revolution?," *Blackwoods* (April 1945): 217-225.

Monnet, Jean, *Memoirs*, (Paris, 1978).

Monroe, E., *Britain's Moment in the Middle East 1914-1971*, (1981).

---, "British Interests in the Middle East," *Middle East Journal* 2, no. 2 (April 1948): 129-146.

---, "Mr. Bevin's Arab Policy," in A. Hourani, ed., *Middle Eastern Affairs*, (1961): 9-48.

Montgomery, Viscount of Alamein, *The Memoirs of Field Marshal Montgomery*, (1960).

Morgan, K., *Labour in Power 1945-1951*, (1984).

Morley, John, *Politics and History*, (1914).

Moore, R. J., *Escape from Empire*, (Oxford, 1983).

---, "Mountbatten, India and the Commonwealth," *Journal of Commonwealth and Comparative Politics* 19 (1981): 5-43.

Morris, James, *Pax Britannica*, (1968).

Morrison, Herbert, *An Autobiography*, (1960).

---, *Prospects and Policies*, (Cambridge, 1943).

---, *What are we Fighting for?*, (1939).

Mosely, Phillip E., "Dismemberment of Germany," *Foreign Affairs* 28 (1950): 486-498.

---, "The Occupation of Germany," *Foreign Affairs* 28 (1950): 580-604.

Mountbatten, L.A.F.V.N., *Speeches*, (New Delhi, 1949).

---, *Time Only to Look Forward*, (1949).

Moynihan, M., *People at War 1939-1945*, (1974).

Mumford, *Programme for Survival*, (1946).

Murphy, John Thomas, *Labour's Big Three*, (1948).

Murphy, R., *Diplomat Among Warriors*, (1964).

Murphy, Ray, *The Life and Times of Rear Admiral the Earl Mountbatten of Burma*, (1948).

Murray, Arthur C., *Reflections on Some Aspects of British Foreign Policy Between the World Wars*, (Edinburgh, 1946).

Needham, Joseph, *History is on Our Side*, (1946).

Nehru, J., *The Discovery of India*, (New York, 1946).

Nicholas, N. G., *Britain and the United States*, (1963).

Nicolson, Nigel, ed., *Harold Nicolson: Diaries and Letters 1939-1945*, (1967).

Nicolson, Sir Harold, "Democratic Diplomacy," *United Empire* 37 (1946): 119.

Nilson, S. S., "Measurement and Models in the Study of Stability," *World Politics* 20, no. 1 (October 1967): 1-29.

Northedge, F. S., *Descent from Power*, (1974).

---, *The Foreign Policies of the Powers*, (1974, 2 ed).

O'Malley, Sir O., *The Phantom Caravan*, (1955).

Orwell, George, *England, Your England and Other Essays*, (1953).

---, *The English People*, (1947).

---, "Riding Down from Bangor," *Tribune* (22 November 1946).

Ovendale, R., "Britain, the United States and the Cold War in South-East Asia 1949-1950," *International Affairs* 58 (1982): 447-464.

---, "Britain, the USA and the European Cold War 1945-1948," *History* 67 (1982): 217-236.

---, *The English Speaking Alliance: Britain, the United States, the Dominions and the Cold War 1945-1951*, (1985).

---, ed., *The Foreign Policy of the British Labour Governments 1945-1951*, (Leicester, 1984).

---, "The Palestine Policy of the British Labour Government 1945-1946," *International Affairs* 59 (1979): 409-431.

---, "The Palestine Policy of the British Labour Government 1947: The Decision to Withdraw," *International Affairs* 56 (1980): 73-93.

---, "The South African Policy of the British Labour Government 1947-1951," *International Affairs* 59 (1983): 41-58.

Owen, David, "Where Now Is Britain," *Canadian Historical Review* (September 1945).

Padover, Saul L., "America and Europe," *Social Research* 17 (December 1950): 403-416.

Page, Sir Arthur, "Wake Up England," *National Review* (November 1945): 386-394.

Pakenham, Frank, *Born to Believe*, (1953).

---, "Standards of British Foreign Policy," *Dublin Review* (April 1945): 171-180

Parker, Ralph, *Plot Against Peace*, (Moscow, 1949).

---, *The Soviet Union Kept Me Young*, (Moscow, 1966).

Parliamentary Debates, Annual volumes for House of Commons and House of Lords.

Partridge, P. H., *Consent and Consensus*, (1971).

Peele, Gillian, and Chris Cook, *The Politics of Reappraisal 1918-1939*, (1976).

Pelling, Henry, *America and the British Left*, (New York, 1957).

---, *Britain and the Second World War*, (1970).

---, "The 1945 General Election Reconsidered," *Historical Journal* 23, no. 2 (June 1980): 399-414.

Pentland, C., *International Theory and European Integration*, (1973).

Petersen, N., "Britain, Scandinavia and the North Atlantic Treaty 1948-1949," *Review of International Studies* 8 (1982): 251-268.

Peterson, M. D., *Both Sides of the Curtain*, (1950).

Petrie, Sir C., *The Carlton Club*, (1972).

Pfau, R., "Containment in Iran 1946: The Shift to an Active Policy," *Diplomatic History* 1 (1979): 359-372.

Pick, Frederick W., *Peacemaking in Perspective from Potsdam to Paris*, (Oxford, 1950).

Pickles, Dorothy M., *French Foreign Policy and Franco-British Misunderstandings*, (1966).

Pickthorn, K., "Philosophy and Principles," in Sydney D. Barley, ed. *The British Party System*, (1952).

Pierre, A. J., *Nuclear Politics: The British Experience with an Independant Strategic Force 1939-1970*, (1972).

Pimlott, Ben, *Hugh Dalton*, (1985).

Platt, D. C., *Finance, Trade and Politics in British Forign Policy 1815-1914*, (Oxford, 1968).

Plumb, J. H., *Churchill: Four Faces and the Man*, (1969).

---, *The Development of the British Economy 1914-1950*, (1960).

Pool, Ithiel de Sola, *The Prestige Papers: A Survey of their Editorials*, (Stanford, Conn., 1952).

---, *Symbols of Internationalism*, (Stanford, Conn., 1951).

Porter, B., *Critics of Empire: British Radical Attitudes to Colonialism in Africa 1895-1914*, (1968).

---, *The Lion's Share*, (1976).

Price, Richard N., *An Imperial War and the British Working Class*, (1972).

Pritt, D. N., *The Autobiography of D. N. Pritt*, 3 volumes (1965).

---, *The Labour Government 1945-1951*, (1963).

Puckler, Count, *How Strong is Britain*, (1939).

Quayle, Eric, *The Collector's Book of Boys' Stories*, (1973).

Raczynski, Count Edward, *In Allied London*, (1962).

Rapaport, A., *The Big Two*, (1970).

Reed, Bruce, and G. Williams, *Dennis Healey and the Policies of Power*, (1971).

Reid, E., *Time of Fear and Hope: The Making of the North Atlantic Treaty 1947-1949*, (Toronto, 1977).

Renier, G. J., *The English: Are they Human*, (1931).

Roberts, F. K., "Ernest Bevin as Foreign Secretary" in R. Ovendale, ed., *The Foreign Policy of the British Labour Governments, 1945-1951*, (Leicester, 1984).

Roberts, H. L., and P. A. Wilson, *Britain and the United States: Problems in Cooperation*, (1953).

Robertson, Michael, *Beyond the Sunset*, (New York, 1950).

Robinson, Ronald, and John Gallagher, *Africa and the Victorians*, (1961).

Robson, W. A., ed., *The Civil Service in Britain and France*, (1956).

Rochefort, Robert, *Robert Schuman*, (Paris, 1968).

Roosevelt, Elliott, *As He Saw It*, (New York, 1946).

Rose, C. Richard, *Politics in England*, (1965).

---, *The Relation of Socialist Principles to British Labour Foreign Policy 1945-1951*, unpublished D. Phil thesis, Oxford University, (1959).

Rose, Lisle A., *Dubious Victory*, (Kent, Ohio, 1973).

Rosecrance, Richard, *Defence of the Realm*, (New York, 1968).

Rosenau, J. N., ed., *Linkage Politics*, (New York, 1969).

---, *Public Opinion and Foreign Policy*, (New York, 1961).

Rosenweig, Linda W., "The Abdication of Edward VIII," *Journal of British Studies* 14, no. 2 (1975): 102-119.

Roskill, Stephen, *Hankey: Man of Secrets*, Volume 3 (1978).

Rothwell, V. H., *Britain and the Cold War 1941-1947*, (1982).

Rowntree, B. S., and G. R. Lavers, *English Life and Leisure*, (1951).

Rowse, A. L., *Appeasement: A Study in Political Decline*, (New York, 1963).

---, *The English Spirit*, (1945).

Royal Institute of International Affairs, *Britain in Western Europe*, (1956).

---, *British Interests in the Mediterranean and Middle East*, (1958).

---, *British Security*, (1946).

---, *Nationalism*, (1939).

---, *Political and Strategic Interests of the United Kingdom*, (1940).

---, *United Kingdom Policy*, (1950).

Rubin, B., *The Great Powers in the Middle East 1941-1947: The Road to the Cold War*, (1980).

Russell, A. G., *Colour, Race and Empire*, (1945).

Russett, Bruce M., *Community and Contention: Britain and America in the Twentieth Century*, (Cambridge, Mass., 1963).

---, *Trends in World Politics*, (New York, 1965).

Ryder, Judith, and Harold Silver, *Modern English Society*, (1970).

Sachar, H. M., *Europe Leaves the Middle East*, (New York, 1972).

Sainsbury, K., "British Policy and German Unity at the End of the Second World War," *English Historical Review* 94 (1979): 786-804.

---, "The Second Wartime Alliance" in N. Waites, ed., *Troubled Neighbours*, (1971).

Santayana, George, *Soliloquies in England*, (1922).

Schulyer, R. L., *The Fall of the Old Colonial System*, (1946).

Schuman, Robert, *Pour L'Europe*, (Paris, 1963).

Scott, J. F., *The Menace of Nationalism in Education*, (1926).

Seeley, J. R., *The Expansion of England*, (1883).

Selby, Sir Walford, "The Foreign Office," *Nineteenth Century* (July 1945): 42-52.

Semmel, B., *Imperialism and Social Reform*, (1960).

Sencourt, R., "New Trends in Diplomacy," *Quarterly Review* (July 1945): 281-295.

Senelick, Laurence, "Politics as Entertainment: Victorian Music Hall Songs," *Victorian Studies* 19, no. 2, (December 1975): 149-180.

Shanks, M., *The Stagnant Society: A Warning*, (1961).

---, and J. Lambert, *Britain and the New Europe*, (1962).

Shannon, H. A., "The Sterling Balances of the Sterling Area 1939-1949," *Economic Journal* 60, no. 3 (1950): 531-551.

Shaw, E. D., *British Socialist Approaches to International Affairs 1945-1951*, unpublished D. Phil thesis, Leeds University, (1974).

Shepherd, Robert J., *Public Opinion and European Integration*, (Farnborough, 1975).

Sherwood, Robert E., *Roosevelt and Hopkins*, (New York, 1950).

Shils, E. A., "Britain and the World," *Review of Politics* 7 (1945): 505-524.

Shinwell, Emanuel, *Conflict without Malice*, (1955).

---, *I've Lived Through It All*, (1973).

---, *Lead With the Left: My First Ninety-Six Years*, (1981).

---, *When the Men Come Home*, (1944).

Shlaim, Avi, Peter Jones, and Keith Sainsbury, *British Foreign Secretaries Since 1945*, (1977).

Shonfield, Andrew, *British Economic Policy Since the War*, (1958).

---, "The Pursuit of Prestige," *Encounter* 8 (January 1957): 38.

Singh, A. I., "Imperial Defence and the Transfer of Power in India 1946-1947," *International Historical Review* 4 (1982): 568-588.

Sissons, Michael, and P. French, eds., *The Age of Austerity*, (1963).

Sitwell, Sir Osbert, *The Scarlet Tree*, (1946).

Smith, Paul, ed., *The Historian and Film*, (Cambridge, 1976).

Smith, R., and J. Zametica, "The Cold Warrior: Clement Attlee Reconsidered 1945-47," *International Affairs* 61, no. 2 (1985).

Snape, R. A., *Britain and the Empire 1867-1945*, (1946).

Snyder, William P., *The Politics of British Defence Policy 1945-1962*, (1964).

Soustelle, J., *Envers et Contre Tout*, 2 volumes (Paris 1950).

Spaak, Paul-Henri, *Combats Inacheves de l'Independance a l'Alliance*, (Brussels, 1969).

Springhall, John O., "The Rise and Fall of Henty's Empire," *Times Literary Supplement*, 3 October 1968, 1105-1106.

---, *Youth, Empire and Society*, (1977).

Sprout, H., and M. Sprout, "The Dilemma of Rising Demands and Insufficient Resources," *World Politics* 20, no. 4 (July 1968): 660-693.

---, "Retreat from World Power," *World Politics* 15, no.4 (1963): 655-688.

Stahl, Kathleen, *The Metropolitan Organization of British Colonial Trade*, (1952).

Stanley, Oliver, "Our Colonial Empire: The Next Chapter," *United Empire* 36 (1945): 216-220.

Starr, Mark, *Lies and Hate in Education*, (1929).

Steiner, Zara, *Britain and the Origins of the First World War*, (1977).

---, *The Foreign Office and Foreign Policy 1898-1914*, (Cambridge, 1969).

Stephens, M., *Ernest Bevin: Unskilled Labourer and World Statesman, 1881-1951*, (1981).

Stettinius, E. R., *Roosevelt and the Russians*, (Garden City, N.J., 1949).

Stevenson, John, and Chris Cook, *The Slump: Society and Politics during the Depression*, (1977).

Stimson, H. L., and Bundy McGeorge, *On Active Service in Peace and War*, (New York, 1948).

Stitt, George M. S., *Under Cunningham's Command*, (1944).

Stoetzel, J., "The Evolution of French Opinion," in D. Lerner and R. Aron, eds., *France Defeats EDC*, (New York, 1957).

Strachey, John, *The Coming Struggle for Power*, (1933).

---, *End of Empire*, (1959).

Strang, Lord, *The Foreign Office*, (1955).

---, "The Formation and Control of Foreign Policy," *Durham University Journal* 49, no.2 (June 1957): 98-108.

---, *Home and Abroad*, (1956).

Strange, Susan, *Sterling and British Policy*, (1971).

Taylor, A.J.P., *Englishmen and Others*, (1956).

Tedder, Sir A. W., *With Prejudice*, (1966).

Terraine, John, *The Life and Times of Lord Mountbatten*, (1968).

Thomas H., *The Establishment: A Symposium*, (1959).

Thomas, Hugh, *John Strachey*, (1973).

Thompson, Neville, *The Anti-Appeasers*, (Oxford, 1971).

Thomson, D., E. Meyer, and A. Briggs, *Patterns of Peacemaking*, (1946).

Thorne, Christopher, *Allies of a Kind*, (1978).

---, *The Limits of Foreign Policy*, (1972).

Thornton, A. P., *For the File on Empire*, (1968).

---, *The Habit of Authority*, (1966).

---, *The Imperial Idea and its Enemies*, (1959).

Thurtle, Ernest, *Time's Winged Chariot: Memories and Comments*, (1945).

Titmuss, Richard, *Problems of Social Policy*, (1950).

Toynbee, Arnold, ed., *Hitler's Europe--Survey of International Affairs 1939-1946*, (1954).

---, "The International Outlook," *International Affairs* 23, no. 4 (1947): 463-476.

Trevelyan, Julian, *Indigo Days*, (1957).

Truman, Harry S, *Memoirs," Volume 2, "Years of Trial and Hope*, (New York, 1956).

Tucker, William R., *The Attitude of the British Labour Party Towards European and Collective Security Problems*, (Geneva, 1950).

Underhill, Frank H., "Trends in American Foreign Policy," *University of Toronto Quarterly* (April 1944): 295.

United Kingdom, Central Office of Information, *British Foreign Policy: A Brief Collection of Fact and Quotation*, (1963)

---, *The Cinema and the Public*, (1946).

United Kingdom Parliamentary Papers, *Statistical Material Presented During the Washington Negotiations*, (CMD 6706, 1945); *Broadcasting Policy*, (CMD 6852, 1946); *Central Organization for Defence*, (CMD 6923, 1946); *Statement on the Economic Conditions Affecting Relations Between Employers and Workers*, (CMD 7018, 1947); *Economic Survey 1947*, (CMD 7046, 1947); and *The Colonial Empire 1939-1947*, (CMD 7167, 1947).

Van der Beugel, E. H., *From Marshall Aid to Atlantic Partnership*, (Amsterdam, 1966).

Vanderschmidt, Fred, *What the English Think of Us*, (New York, 1948).

Vaughan, R., *Post-War Integration in Europe*, (1976).

Vernon, Betty, *Ellen Wilkinson*, (1982).

Viorst, M., *Hostile Allies*, (New York, 1965).

Vital, David, *The Making of British Foreign Policy*, (1968).

Voigt, F. A., "Opinion and Policy," *Nineteenth Century* (October 1945): 145-155.

Waites, N., *Troubled Neighbours*, (1971).

Wallace, L. P., and W. C. Askew, eds., *Power, Public Opinion and Diplomacy*, (Durham, 1959).

Wallace, W., *The Foreign Policy Process in Britain*, (1976).

Waltz, Kenneth N., "British Defence and Alliance Strategy: The Quandary of a Middle Power," *Polity* 3, no. 2 (Winter 1970): 141-174.

---, *Foreign Policy and Democratic Politics: The American and British Experience*, (1968).

Warner, G., "The Reconstruction and Defence of Western Europe after 1945," in N. Waites, ed., *Troubled Neighbours*, (1971).

Warner, Oliver, *Cunningham of Hyndhope*, (1967).

Watt, D. C., "The British Cold War," *The Listener* (1 June 1978): 711-712.

Welles, Sumner, *Seven Decisions that Shaped History*, (New York, 1950).

Weymouth, Anthony, *Journal of the War Years*, 2 volumes (Worcester, 1948).

Wheeler-Bennett, Sir John, *Friends, Enemies and Sovereigns*, (1976).

---, *King George VI*, (1958).

---, and A. Nichols, *The Semblance of Peace*, (1972).

Wilkinson, Ellen, *The Town that was Murdered*, (1939).

Willcox, William D., "Forces of Change in the English Speaking World," *Yale Review* (Autumn 1943): 24-27.

Williams, Francis, *Ernest Bevin: Portrait of a Great Englishman*, (1952).

---, *A Pattern of Rulers*, (1965).

---, *Press, Parliament and People*, (1946).

---, *The Triple Challenge*, (1948).

Williams, Philip, ed., *The Diary of Hugh Gaitskell 1945-1956*, (1983).

Williamson, James A., *Great Britain and the Empire*, (1945).

---, *The Ocean in English History*, (Oxford, 1948).

Wimperis, H. E., *World Power and Atomic Energy*, (1946).

Winant, John G., *A Letter from Grosvenor Square*, (1947).

Winterton, Earl, *Fifty Tumultuous Years*, (1955).

Winterton, Paul, *Report on Russia*, (1946).

Wittkopf, Eugene R., *Faces of Internationalism: Public Opinion and American Foreign Policy*, (London, 1990).

Wood, Jarvis H., *Let the Great Story be Told*, (1946).

Woodward, Sir E. Ll., *History of England*, (1947).

---, *Short Journey*, (Oxford, 1942).

Woolf, Leonard, *Downhill all the Way: An Autobiography of the Years 1919-1939*, (1967).

---, *Foreign Policy: The Labour Party's Dilemma*, (1947).

---, *The Future of International Government*, (1940).

---, "The International Post-War Settlement," *Fabian Publications Research Series* 85 (1944).

Woolton, Lord, "A Charter for Britain at Peace," *London Quarterly World Affairs* (October 1945): 201-205.

Wrench, J. E., *Geoffrey Dawson and Our Times*, (1955).

Wyatt, Woodrow, *Confessions of an Optimist*, (1985).

---, *Into the Dangerous World*, (1952).

Young, George K., *Masters of Indecision*, (1962).

Young, John W., *Britain, France and the Unity of Europe 1945-1951*, (Leicester, 1984).

Youngson, A. J., *Britain's Economic Growth 1920-1966*, (1967).

Ziegler, Philip, *Mountbatten: The Official Biography*, (1985).

Index

Advisory Committee on Atomic Energy, 135
Afghanistan, 90
Alanbrooke, 1st Viscount, 119, 121, 142
Alexander, Albert, 11-12, 21, 23, 25, 53, 62, 65, 67, 70, 72, 75, 91-92, 96, 98, 119, 124, 129, 140-141
Allport, Gordon, 9-10
Altrincham, 1st Baron, 77f
Amery, Leopold, 38
Anderson, John, 133
Ashton-Gwatkin, Frank, 18-19, 63
Atomic Bomb, 6, 132-137
Attitudes: change, 13; definition, 9-10; formation, 10-11
Attlee, Bernard, 52
Attlee, Clement, 6, 11, 14-15, 20-23, 25, 52-53, 55, 62, 65, 67-69, 72-73, 75, 77, 81-82, 90-97, 99, 111, 115, 118, 120, 122-125, 127-128, 133, 136, 138-141, 143-144, 146-147

Baden Powell, 1st Baron, 50
Barclay, Roderick, 24, 33-34, 36, 98, 141
Barker, Ernest, 52
Baruch Plan, 132
Beaverbrook, 1st Baron, 119
Belgium, 144, 149
Bevan, Aneurin, 111, 146
Beveridge Report, 83
Bevin, Ernest, 6, 11, 13, 18, 20-25, 27, 31-39, 47, 53, 56, 62-63, 65, 67, 69-75, 82, 84, 91-94, 97-99, 109-111, 118, 120-122, 124-125, 128-132, 135, 138, 139, 141, 143, 146-147, 149

Bevin, Florence, 36
Bevin, Queenie, 36
Blackett, Patrick, 135, 137
Boer War, 45, 47-48, 52-53
Boys' Brigade, 50
Boy Scout Movement, 50, 52
Bretton Woods Institutions, 63
Briand, Aristide, 144, 147
British Empire and Commonwealth, 26-27, 48, 109, 116-122, 129, 131-132, 138, 141-142, 146, 162
British Institute of Public Opinion, 83
Bryant, Arthur, 47
Burke, Edmund, 23
Burma, 124, 126
Butler, Nevile, 18
Byrnes, James F. 33, 136

Cadogan, Alexander, 18, 25, 34, 65, 70-71, 92
Canada, 144
Carnegie Foundation for International Peace, 51
Carr, Edward, 77
Churchill, Winston, 6, 39, 64, 66, 68, 72, 94, 116, 123-124, 132, 156
Chuter-Ede, James, 37, 128
Clarke, H. O., 127
Clarke, Kerr, A. K., 18
Clive in India, 49
Cognitive Dissonance, 13, 97
Connel, John, 19
Combined Development Trust, 133
Combined Policy Committee, 133
Contrast in Records, 5
Cooper, Duff, 20
Coudenhove, de Kalergi, Count, 144

Council of Europe, 145, 147, 150
Creech-Jones, Arthur, 117
Crimean War, 45
Cripps, R. Stafford, 21, 23, 25, 53, 56, 90, 119, 123-124, 146
Crombie, James, 18
Cunningham, Andrew, 71, 96, 131, 141-142
Curtis, Lionel, 146
Curzon, First Marquess, 38, 47, 123

Dalton, Hugh, 15, 21, 23, 25, 35, 39, 56, 63, 67, 76, 82-83, 89-93, 98, 100, 108-109, 111, 119, 121, 129-130, 138-139, 141
Darby, Philip, 142
Defence Committee, 21-22, 111, 129, 142
Denmark, 149
Derwent, 3rd Baron, 92
Dixon, Piers, 18, 25, 33, 36, 39, 92, 128
Donnelly, J. C., 127
Dunkirk, 66, 75-76, 161

Economic Consequences of War, 3-5
Eden, Anthony, 6, 18, 38, 63, 71, 145
Egypt, 92-93, 116, 137, 140, 142. See also Middle East.
El Alamein, 142
Elizabeth I, 38
Emerson, Ralph Waldo, 67
Enemy Coast Ahead, 65
Epstein, Leon, 69
European Coal and Steel Community, 150
European Defence Community, 150
European Economic Community, 150

European Integration, 14, 84, 144-150
European Recovery Programme, 127, 145
External Relations Committee, 21-22

Farouk, King, 77
Foreign Office Personnel, 13
Foreign Policy Decision-Making Process, 17, 23
France, 135, 137, 144
Frankel, Joseph, 84
Frankfurter, Felix, 31
Franks, Oliver, 11, 112, 54, 121

Gallup Polls, 10
George VI, 39, 64, 99-100
Germany, 37, 74, 83, 109, 135, 144-145, 149
Gibson, Guy, 65
Gladwyn Jebb, Hugh, 10, 18, 27, 32, 38, 54, 147
Gloucester, Duke of, 39
Goldberg, Alfred, 136
Gowing, Margaret, 137
Greece, 6, 70, 90, 93, 95-97, 107, 109, 129, 137-139
Grey of Fallodon, 1st Viscount, 31
Groom, Arthur, 136
Guilty Men, 5

Hall, George, 21-22, 96, 139
Halloran, J. D., 11, 13
Hall-Patch, Edmund, 18
Hankey, Maurice, 120
Hardie, Keir, 31
Harvey, O. C., 18
Henderson, Nicholas, 33
Henty, George, 11, 49-50, 53
Hobson, John, 117
Hopkins, Harry, 127

Howe, Robert, 18
Huizinga, J. H., 100

India, 6, 12, 82-83, 93, 107, 122-
126, 139, 141, Quit India
Movement, 123
Iraq, 109, 116, 139-140
Italy, 144, Italian Colonies, 96

Japan, 132
Johnson, Arthur, 52
Joliot-Curie, Frederic, 137

Kelly, David, 12, 54, 110
Kenya, 139
Keynes, John Maynard, 15, 66, 74,
89-91, 109
Kierkegaard, Soren, 14
King, Mackenzie, 133
Kipling, Rudyard, 11, 49, 51-53
Kirkpatrick, Ivonne, 18, 34

Labour Party Foreign Policy Revolt
1946, 6
Lapie, Pierre, 56
Laski, Harold, 31
Lawson, John, 21-22
Libya, 137
Liddel Hart, Basil, 109, 138-139,
143
Lockhart, Bruce, 31
Luxemburg, 144, 149

Macaulay, Thomas, 46, 53
McCall, Alec, 36
McDonald, Iverach, 118
Mackay, Ronald, 146
Mckenzie, Grant, 15, 26
McMahon Act, 133-134
MacMillan, Harold, 112
MacNeill, Hector, 21, 147
Malaya, 121
Mallet, Victor, 35

Marshall Aid, 145
Martin, Kingsley, 15
Marwick, Arthur, 163
Marx, Karl, 117, 163
Mary, Queen, 39
Massey, Ben, 36
May, Alan Nunn, 133
Mayhew, Christopher, 21, 147-148
Middle East, 6, 20, 70, 91, 95,
129-130, 138-143, 146
Milton, John, 67
Montgomery, Bernard 130, 141
Morrison, Herbert, 21, 25, 53, 55-
56, 117, 119, 128
Mountbatten, 1st Earl, 125
Munich, 61
Music Halls, 45, 53

Netherlands, 144, 149
Newton, Basil, 32
Noel Baker, Philip, 21, 62
North Atlantic Treaty Organization,
144, 146, 150
Norway, 149

Organization for European
Economic Cooperation, 144-146
Orwell, George, 50

Pakenham, Francis, 11, 69
Pakistan, 123
Palestine, 83, 93, 107, 109, 137-
138
Palmerston, 3rd Viscount, 17, 27,
49, 56
Paris Peace Conference 1946, 22
Penney, William, 135
Persia, 139
Petersen, Maurice, 18, 130
Pethick Lawrence, Frederick, 124
Phillips, Tom, 22
Poland, 34
Portugal, 149

Portal, Frederick, 96
Potsdam Conference 1945, 34, 92, 128
Public Schools, 51

Rhodes, Cecil, 46
Robbins, Lionel, 83
Robson, William, 82
Rommel, Erwin, 142
Ronald, Nigel, 14, 18, 70, 149
Roosevelt, Franklin D., 132
Royal Institute for International Affairs, 147
Russia (See Soviet Union)

San Francisco Conference 1945, 25, 70
Sarawak, 6, 122
Sargent, Orme, 18, 23, 25, 55, 83
Scandinavia, 110, 130, 144
Scott, David, 18
Scott, Captain Robert, 48
Shills, Edward, 66
Shinwell, Emmanuel, 21, 53, 77, 119
Smith, William, 50
Social Darwinism, 46
Soviet Union, 6, 11, 25, 32-34, 70-71, 93, 95, 110, 126, 128-131, 135-139, 145-147, 149, 161-162
Spain, 149
Spencer, Herbert, 46
Sport, 110-111
Stansgate, 1st Viscount, 21
Statute of Westminster, 116
Steering Committee on International Organizations, 20
Stimson, Henry, 64
Strachey, John, 119
Strang, William, 18-20, 35, 38, 54, 148-149
Strategic Images, 15

Tedder, Arthur, 95-96, 142
Templewood, 1st Viscount, 109
The Times, 61
Third Force, 146-148
Tizard, Henry, 112, 119
Toynbee, Arnold, 18
Treaty of Brussels 1948, 144, 146, 150
Treaty of Dunkirk 1947, 144, 146, 150
Treaty of Rome 1957, 150
Troutbeck, John, 150
Truman, Harry S, 133, 136
Turkey, 70, 90, 97, 107, 110, 129, 139

United Nations Organization, 25, 63, 68, 92, 128, 131, 140
United States of America, 6, 25-27, 47, 74-75, 90, 93, 107, 109-110, 120, 124, 126-128, 130-135, 144-147, 161-162
Us and Our Empire, 49

Warner, G. F. A., 18, 149
Wavell, 1st Earl, 123
Webster, Charles, 18
Welldon, James, 51
West Indies, 111
Wheeler Bennett, John, 55
Williams Francis, 120, 146, 153
Wilmot, John, 21-22
Wilson, Harold, 112
Wolsey, Thomas, 32
Wyatt, Woodrow, 39, 99

Young, George, 20
Younger, Kenneth, 82
Your M. P., 5
Youth Clubs, 50

Zilliacus, Konni, 31, 94-95

About the Author

MICHAEL BLACKWELL is an economist and the resident representative of the International Monetary Fund in the Republic of Moldova.